Peace at the Last

Leading funerals well

Robert Atwell

CANTERBURY PRESS

Norwich

© Robert Atwell 2014

First published in 2014 by the Canterbury Press Norwich
Editorial office
3rd Floor, Invicta House,
108–114 Golden Lane,
London EC1Y 0TG.

Canterbury Press is an imprint of Hymns Ancient & Modern Ltd
(a registered charity)
13A Hellesdon Park Road, Norwich,
Norfolk, NR6 5DR, UK

www.canterburypress.co.uk

British Library Cataloguing in Publication data

A catalogue record for this book is available
from the British Library

978 1 84825 666 8

Typeset by Manila Typesetting Company
Printed and bound in Great Britain by
CPI Group (UK) Ltd, Croydon

Contents

About this book

This book has its origins in a series of meetings and conversations about the changing nature of funeral ministry that took place in Cheshire and south Manchester between April 2012 and December 2013. For generations a Christian funeral was the default option of the majority of the British population, and the bulk of funerals were Anglican. A funeral was normally conducted by the vicar either in the parish church, followed by burial or cremation, or entirely at the local cemetery or crematorium chapel. This pattern is no longer the norm. The last 40 years have seen huge changes. Society today is more diverse, with significant populations of those of other faiths and an increasing number of people who claim to have no faith at all. According to funeral directors, in some urban areas civil or humanist services now account for between 12 and 15 per cent of funerals, though a few undertakers give a figure as high as 30 per cent. Whatever the precise number, it is clear that nationally the number of Christian funerals is in decline.

In an attempt to understand more about what is happening, the University of Chester conducted a research project in 2012 into the experiences of funeral directors, clergy and bereaved families in and around Warrington, an area that ecclesiastically straddles the Dioceses of Chester and Liverpool. In parallel with this project the bishops and archdeacons of the Diocese of Chester hosted a series of meetings with funeral directors to listen to their concerns, to reflect with them on the expectations of their clients and to rebuild a sense of partnership, not least with the implementation of the new Ecclesiastical Fees (Amendment) Measure

2011, which came into force in January 2013 and changed the procedure for the payment and ownership of funeral fees. Sadly only half of the funeral directors invited either responded to the invitation or agreed to meet. In itself it was an indication of the underlying tension that sometimes exists between the Church of England and some funeral directors, which in certain quarters can amount to estrangement. Those who did participate in the meetings were primarily independent funeral directors and, it should be noted, were hugely appreciative of the opportunity to talk.

As a result of these consultations a parallel series of meetings was held in 2013 across the Diocese of Chester to which clergy, readers authorized to take funerals and parish administrators were invited. The purpose of the meetings was to listen to concerns and to give feedback from the funeral directors and the University of Chester funeral project. The conversations that emerged during these meetings were robust, stimulating, insightful and on occasion deeply moving. They released a surge of energy to improve our funeral ministry of which this book is the fruit.

Drawing upon the wealth of pastoral experience that was shared, and as a contribution to the National Funeral Project,[1] this guide seeks to distil good practice and disseminate it with a view to raising the quality of funeral services, particularly those conducted by Anglican ministers. It offers an overview of the changing landscape of death, together with some practical advice about shaping funeral services to meet the expectations of a new generation. It looks at the place of music and song in funerals, the role of preaching, the importance of investing in good, professional relationships with local funeral directors, and the pastoral care of the bereaved. Included in the appendices is a selection of readings that can be used in the context of funerals and memorial services as a supplement to biblical readings.

This guide also contains information about what happens when someone dies, from a medical and legal point of view. In this context

---

1 Funded by the Archbishops' Council of the Church of England, this research project is looking at a range of emerging questions about death and the changing face of funerals in England.

I am immensely grateful to the Very Reverend Professor Gordon McPhate for his medical knowledge and to Elizabeth Pygott, Assistant Coroner in the West London Jurisdiction, for her legal knowledge. I am also indebted to Christopher Hill, formerly Bishop of Guildford, for his grasp of Canon Law and his permission to quote from his note on the disposal of ashes; to Pauline Green for sharing her wisdom accumulated over many years as a funeral director; to Patrick Dearnley for information about the growth of funeral homes; and to Jenny Bridgman for her research into humanist funerals.

Finally I wish to record my gratitude to my former colleagues in the Diocese of Chester: Peter Forster, Keith Sinclair, Ian Bishop, Michael Gilbertson, Ian Rumsey, Richard Burton, John Varty and, finally, Margaret Andrews, my PA, whose patience seemingly had no bounds.

Robert Atwell

The changing landscape of death

No man is an island, entire of itself; every man is a piece of the
continent, a part of the main . . . Any man's death diminishes
me, because I am involved in mankind. And therefore never
send to know for whom the bell tolls; it tolls for thee.

John Donne (1572–1631)[1]

Like most people of my generation, I entered adult life with little contact or understanding of death. Death happened to other
people. True, aged 15 I had attended my grandmother's funeral.
Ensconced in the back of the undertaker's limousine, I remember spotting the priest hastily stub out his cigarette when he saw
the cortège approaching the crematorium chapel ahead of sched-
ule. Moments later he reappeared in cassock, surplice and purple
stole, his face suitably composed into an expression of professional empathy. I remember too my grandfather sobbing, 'Don't
leave me, Ede. Don't leave me', as my grandmother's coffin glided
along the catafalque and disappeared from view. As we left the
chapel the priest grasped my grandfather's hand and said, 'Don't
worry, Mr Atwell. You'll be with her soon.' Even at 15 I knew it
was a crass thing to say.

I emerged into the afternoon sunshine equipped with the knowledge that death is irrevocable and that the pain of parting can be
searing. But that was as far as things went. I had never been with
anyone when they died and I had never seen, let alone touched, a
dead body. Death was still an unknown quantity, the preserve of the
old and frail, a world peopled by doctors, clergy and undertakers.

---

1 *Devotions upon Emergent Occasions, and Several Steps in my Sick-
ness*, Meditation 17.

That was why, seven years later at the age of 22 and now en route to theological college, I wrote to St Christopher's Hospice in south London to offer my services as a volunteer. My offer was accepted, and during the long vacation I worked partly as a lay chaplain and partly as an auxiliary nurse on one of the wards.

There were many life-transforming encounters that summer. I remember a woman in her late thirties and in the final stages of breast cancer. Bald from chemotherapy and bloated from the effects of steroids, Frances did not look like the handsome woman who beamed out at me from the family snapshot that had pride of place on her bedside locker. Over the days and weeks of that long hot summer I got to know her well. I heard her love for her husband, her children and parents, and her anxiety about how they would cope with her death. I found her openness and trust in me moving, but it also made me somewhat blasé. Overnight I thought I knew it all. As I was tidying her bed one morning she said, 'Death may be routine to you, Robert, but it's new to me. You see, I've never died before.'

The early monks who peopled the Egyptian and Palestinian deserts in the fourth and fifth centuries talked of *compunctio cordis*. Compunction was a medical term of the Roman doctors designating attacks of acute pain, but the Desert Fathers and Mothers applied it to pain of the spirit – 'compunction of the heart'. They used the term to describe a pricking or uneasiness of conscience, a remorse born of penitence, an experience of nakedness before God that makes possible moments of profound disclosure. Falsity is stripped away and suddenly the heart is pierced by a perception of truth that leads to a new quality of inner freedom. That August morning, making Frances's bed, was just such a moment. There have been many others since.

I was with Frances when she died. Her deterioration one Thursday afternoon was swift and, to a degree, unexpected. That evening I handed her husband a final letter she had written in her strong, clear hand. She did not want him to be alone and was confident that God would find him a good woman who could be as good a, if not better, mother to their three children. I studied his face as he read the letter and again later as together we

viewed her body. I remember his silent weeping. I remember too watching him climb into their car, shoulders hunched, clutching a black hospital bag with the bits and pieces that had decorated her room.

Death evokes a variety of responses. They may range from denial, anger, defiance, recognition and fear, through to calm acceptance. With less of life to look forward to, the past comes into sharp relief. Some, like the poet Dylan Thomas, rebel against its encroachment:

Do not go gentle into that good night,
Old age should burn and rave at close of day;
Rage, rage against the dying of the light.[2]

There is a time and a place for anger, particularly when it cuts short the life of a young mother, but there is also a time and a place to go gentle into God's good night.

Frances was the first of many people I have accompanied on their final journey. Some raged 'against the dying of the light'. Some were frightened not of annihilation but of absurdity. For them, death sealed the emptiness of a life not fully lived. Death came too soon, before they could make sense of their life, before they could make one last attempt to give it meaning. Some were vulnerable to attacks of despair in which their sense of the value of all that had gone before drained away. The sting of death was not the loss of life but the loss of meaning. But others, like Frances, were people of faith who died confident in their love of God and of God's love for them.

It is a privilege to prepare someone for their death, to be with them in their last hours and with their family as they mourn their loss, or later to preside at the funeral and support the bereaved in the weeks that follow. Few of us are there for all of these events. Instead we find ourselves part of a network, a link in the human chain of caring. Unless a priest has known the individual or their

---

2 Dylan Thomas (1952), 'Do Not Go Gentle Into That Good Night', *Collected Poems 1934–1952*, London: Dent, p. 116.

family and friends personally, it is likely that he or she will only become involved when the family makes arrangements for the funeral. If the family trusts you, they will open their hearts and homes to you. Done well and handled with sensitivity, they can be brought to a richer understanding of God's gift of life and begin a spiritual journey of their own. It is why funerals are such an important part of our mission and ministry. But attitudes to death and to funerals are changing.

Contrary to what most people imagine, there is no legal requirement to have a funeral at all. Nor does the law stipulate the form a funeral must take or that it should be conducted by a minister of religion. Forty years ago a Christian funeral was the default option of the majority of the population and most funerals were conducted according to the rites of the Church of England. The service was performed by the local vicar either in the parish church, followed by burial or cremation, or else entirely at the cemetery or crematorium chapel. This is no longer the case. In 2002 the government published a White Paper entitled *Civil Registration: Vital Change* that opened the way for people other than clergy to conduct funerals. There is no nationwide collation of statistics on funerals and estimates vary. But according to funeral directors, who in the absence of government statistics are probably best placed to know, in urban areas civil, secular or humanist funerals now account for between 12 and 15 per cent, though a few undertakers give a figure as high as 30 per cent. Whatever the precise number, what is clear is that nationally the number of Christian funerals – and of Anglican funerals in particular – is falling.

The triumph of choice

For much of the last century, aspects of institutional religion have been in decline, at least in Britain and Europe. Religion has become a leisure activity, something we do in our spare time, an optional extra. To our increasingly not just de-churched but un-churched society, Sunday is special but only as a day for family

and friends, a day for catching up on chores or doing the shopping. Its religious character has been eroded beyond recognition. Life has been privatized along with much else. Choice has become a dominant feature of twenty-first-century living, impacting the type of funeral we want as well as the type of clothes we buy. These days you can have designer coffins as well as designer jeans. The type of music people choose has also broadened considerably. In advance of their funeral, the website Finalfling.com encourages its users to capture and update their 'favourite music on our My Wishes section'. They should 'explain why you picked the piece of music, who it's dedicated to, or where, when, how you would like it played – live, recorded, sing-along, at entry or exit'.

Funerals are increasingly bespoke, tailor-made to fit the requirements of the bereaved or indeed of the deceased. Our generation, accustomed 'to doing its own thing' in every other sphere of life, brings that mindset to bear on how granddad's funeral should be organized. Even when a funeral is conducted by a recognized Christian minister, the content and style of the service can vary hugely. The choice of readings, music, prayers and even the type of hearse is likely to be individualistic. People expect to have whatever they want and can be very eclectic in their tastes.

There have always been those who enjoy flouting convention and rebel against formality, ritual or anything that smacks of institutional religion. Their distaste of solemnity is likely to be directed as much against lugubrious undertakers, dressed in black top hats, parading along the street and pompously bowing to coffins, as against sanctimonious clergymen. The actor and comedian Peter Sellers was determined to have the last laugh at his own funeral and decreed that, as his coffin disappeared from view to be cremated, over the loudspeakers of the crematorium chapel should be played Glenn Miller's 'In the Mood'. Today's rebels, eschewing crematoria and anything that might pollute the atmosphere, are more likely to opt for an alternative funeral, preferring to be buried in a wicker coffin in a woodland glade with a rowan tree for a memorial. So-called green funerals are certainly growing in popularity in our environmentally conscious age. Meanwhile there are still those who like a good show, complete with massive

floral tributes and a horse-drawn hearse. In our island race there will also always be some who choose to have their ashes scattered at sea, and to their number is being added an eccentric few who are paying to have their ashes blasted into outer space. There are even companies that incorporate cremated remains into glass-blown ornaments. It would seem that when it comes to funerals just about anything is possible. It's all happening.

Although the majority of the population remain conventional in their tastes, or at least less esoteric, in terms of any religious awareness that might inform a funeral service, most people inhabit a spiritual fog. The great Christian narrative that shaped the outlook of earlier generations, including an understanding of death, has been discarded. Biblical knowledge is at best rudimentary, at worst non-existent. The rituals of mourning that sustained our grandparents have been jettisoned. There is no longer a common religious language that ministers can use to shape the inchoate beliefs of the bereaved in their struggle for meaning. The comments of the bereaved can vary from 'We know he's still with us', to 'She's gone to be an angel'. It is as if a pseudo-Christian language is evolving to fill the vacuum created by the loss of the biblical vocabulary. There is not even a common musical repertoire to help plug the gap. As a generation we have lost the capacity to lament and we scratch around for words, images and music to express our grief. In today's 'pick 'n' mix' culture, most get by on a diet of half-remembered hymns from schooldays and the odd pearl of homely wisdom gleaned from a magazine in the dentist's waiting room.

Death, multiculturalism and belonging

The decline in the number of Christian funerals is a complex phenomenon that cannot be placed at the door of any one cause. It is a feature of a society that has become diverse, mobile, anonymous and informal. Less and less do particular places, communities and traditions provide the context or form the expectations that shape our lives. People move house, usually for economic reasons. An

unfettered market economy demands mobility, and better and cheaper transport makes it possible. Increased immigration means that the matrix of beliefs, customs, music and ritual that forms Western culture is less monochrome. British culture has diversified and been enriched, though arguably losing coherence in the process.

Jonathan Sacks, the UK's former Chief Rabbi, draws a helpful distinction between multiculturalism and a multi-ethnic society. A multi-ethnic society he welcomes; but multiculturalism, he argues, undermines social cohesion. He distinguishes on the one hand between a country house, 'where every minority is welcome but is a guest', and on the other a hotel where 'nobody is at home [because] it doesn't belong to anyone. We've each got our room and so long as we don't disturb the neighbours we can do whatever we like.' Both, he says, are the poor relation of 'a home which we all build together'. Integrated diversity 'values the dignity of difference'. It seeks 'integration without assimilation'.[3] In Britain today, he laments, we are no longer sure who we are or what we believe, let alone how to build a home together.

As a generation we are certainly less rooted than our grandparents. We are no longer certain where we belong and this is impacting on what happens when someone dies and the rituals that constellate around death. The ancient Greeks had no trouble with belonging. They were proud of their city states and readily identified with their place of birth. Saint Paul, sharing in the Hellenistic culture that pervaded the Mediterranean world, tells us that he was born and brought up in Tarsus. He boasts of his Roman citizenship. He tells us that he is a Hebrew, born of the tribe of Benjamin, and a Pharisee by upbringing (Phil. 3.5). Paul had an instinctive sense of his place in the world. Our medieval forebears had a similar sense of belonging shaped by the land they tilled and the parish in which they worshipped. Above all, they knew that at the end of their lives they would

---

3 *The Times*, London, 19 August 2013; see also Jonathan Sacks (2007), *The Home We Build Together: Recreating Society*, London and New York: Continuum, pp. 13–23.

be buried in the churchyard alongside their relatives and neighbours. The community of the dead, through which they walked
on their way to church every Sunday, fashioned a unique sense
of belonging.

Some of this sensibility transferred to our new industrial towns,
and in Victorian times it was reinforced by a sense of civic pride.
Well into the twentieth century families continued to live in close
proximity to one another, caring for grandchildren and elderly
relatives, often under one roof. In many Asian families this pattern of more than one generation living together persists, but elsewhere it has disappeared, perhaps irrevocably. Family networks
have come under strain and sometimes fractured. More people
are working longer hours or holding down two jobs to secure
a better income. Today fewer people remain in the same job or
stay resident in the same town during their lifetime and, unlike
earlier generations, most no longer know where they will die or
be buried.

It would be some comfort to think that the loss of a sense
of community is predominantly an urban phenomenon, or at
least an inner-city one, but this is not the case. In Middlewich,
a small town in mid Cheshire, an old man died alone and his
body wasn't discovered for some days, and only then because of
the smell. He had no friends or family and rarely went out. And
yet there was a palpable sense of collective guilt that this could
have happened in a small, prosperous Cheshire market town.
The sentiment that 'no one should die alone' was expressed several times to the local parish priest, and yet in an increasingly
anonymous society such events are more common than most of
us like to think.

Joseph Williams, a Roman Catholic parish priest in Bedford-
shire, parked his car outside a supermarket in Houghton Regis in
the days after Christmas to do his weekly shop. In spite of people
constantly coming and going, it would seem that for three days
nobody noticed the priest slumped over his steering wheel, dead,
in spite of the fact that his parish had put out an alert when they
realized that their priest was missing. What kind of society have
we slumped to that a 42-year-old man can die of a heart attack

in a busy supermarket car park and nobody bother to stop their laden trolley and investigate?[4]

The emergence of the term 'bedroom community' among architects and social commentators is another example of dislocation. For some, 'home' is now just the place where you happen to sleep while your real life is elsewhere. To the aspiring young this may sound attractive, except that there is no network of relationships to support you when you are in a crisis or when you are confronted by death. By contrast, as the root of the word 'religion' in the Latin verb 'to bind' reminds us, religion binds us to God and to one another. Religion forges human identity. It is about belonging to a community of faith, not just a 'bedroom community'. It is about having a 'spiritual home' – or should be. The fact that the dead Roman Catholic priest was not noticed by passers-by for three days is unbearably sad.

Taken together, multiculturalism, greater mobility, the exaltation of choice, the diversification and privatization of society, the fragmentation of families and communities, the weakening of religious affiliation, the decline in churchgoing and a crisis in belonging are all factors contributing to the decline in Christian funerals. In rural areas, where a sense of belonging and community is usually stronger, the decline may be less evident. But in urban and inner city areas, where people may have only a tenuous connection to a place and little or no connection to a worshipping community, there is less reason to turn to the church when in need. In an age that values the relational, if there is no known or recognizable human face to personalize an otherwise anonymous institution, it makes little sense to attempt to connect with it in the hour of death.

According to the last National Census, in spite of a reduction in the number of those who describe themselves as 'Christian', the majority of the British population still claims to believe, even if they are not keen on going to church. Where the Church of England has suffered most over the last 20 years has been the loss of what used to be called 'folk religion' or what is nowadays more

---

4 Report in *The Independent*, London, 5 January 2014.

usually referred to as 'cultural Christians' – those on the fringe. They relate to Christianity and its values. They admire the ethos of church schools and the quality of education on offer. They appear in our pews from time to time, perhaps for a Christingle service or Harvest Festival or on Remembrance Sunday. They may even ask for their babies to be baptized, particularly if it increases the chances of their children getting a place in the excellent church school down the road. They are fascinated by the ether of spirituality but tend to be allergic to dogma. Typically they describe themselves as 'spiritual, but not religious'. It is this group that is vulnerable to ticking the box 'No religion' on the national census form, this group that no longer automatically turns to the church to conduct the funerals of friends and relatives, this group that we need to win back urgently as part of our mission. But things are far from straightforward. There are other players in the marketplace competing for their custom.

Funeral celebrants

In recent years a new cadre of 'funeral celebrants' has emerged to cater for those of no faith or who no longer feel at home in church and are ambivalent about organized religion. Titles vary and celebrants may variously describe themselves as civil, universalist, secular or humanist, depending on their approach. Funerals can, of course, be 'self-led', a relative or friend of the family presiding at the ceremony and pressing the button at the crematorium. It is not unknown for funeral directors to double-up as celebrants. For an additional fee, many undertakers are more than happy to preside at a funeral in addition to offering their customary services. The ranks of funeral celebrants may also be swollen in some areas by so-called independent or 'non-denominational ministers'. They describe themselves as Christian but operate outside church structures, usually for financial reasons.

Since April 2002 the Institute of Civil Funerals (IoCF) has sought to train, accredit and support 'civil celebrants' to conduct funeral ceremonies. According to their website, 'A Civil Funeral is

a funeral driven by the wishes, beliefs and values of the deceased and their family, not by the beliefs or ideology of the person conducting the funeral. It sits between a religious service and a humanist funeral.'[5] Working in close co-operation with a funeral director, they seek 'to maintain a high degree of personal involvement with the bereaved family', leading to the creation of a 'life-centred' ceremony. There is no obligation in law, however, for a funeral celebrant to receive training or to join such a professional organization; many do not and prefer to freelance. This lack of accountability is problematic. Unlike the clergy who are accountable to their bishop or other denominational authority for their conduct, many funeral celebrants operate outside any professional structure. Bereaved families are vulnerable, and if a funeral has been mishandled or the relationship of trust between the family and the officiant breaks down, to whom do they complain?

Unlike a civil wedding ceremony where parameters are tightly drawn by the law to exclude religious material, there are no such restrictions for a civil funeral. A civil funeral can have any format. It may and often does contain hymns, psalms and prayers, including the Lord's Prayer if requested by the family. Indeed funeral directors report that some civil funerals incorporate so much religious material that they become virtually indistinguishable from the funerals conducted by Christian ministers, bar the lack of robes! By contrast, a secular or humanist funeral will rigorously exclude all readings from Scripture, hymns and religious imagery.

A civil funeral ceremony can be held in conjunction with a cremation or burial, and can be held at most locations, but not in churches or religious buildings. In the case of burials, a civil funeral can only take place at a non-religious burial ground such as a natural burial ground or a local authority cemetery, not a churchyard. As their publicity states, 'If the person who has died did not regularly attend a place of worship, and either had their own spiritual beliefs, or none at all, you may well feel uncomfortable

---

5 www.iocf.org.uk, accessed October 2013.

with the idea of a full religious ceremony.'[6] It is this pastoral flexibility, perfectly pitched to a constituency that claims to be 'spiritual, but not religious', that is proving so attractive.

Whatever label is used, many funeral celebrants do a more than competent job and – let it be said – earn a comfortable living in the process. Typically they are courteous, efficient, well-turned-out, professional in their dealings and totally focused on the needs of the bereaved. One civil celebrant, it was reported, always gives the family a bound copy of the order of service she has led as a memorial of the occasion. Most celebrants have their own publicity and websites, which makes them readily accessible in an internet-savvy age to those on the fringe. Some have even entered into business partnerships with local funeral directors and are 'on their books'. Unlike clergy, for whom funeral ministry is just one aspect of the job, funeral celebrants are focused on this one thing and are always available at the end of a phone. They know that funeral directors are under pressure from bereaved families to fix the date and time of a funeral, and that undertakers have to juggle slots and availability with crematoria or cemetery officials. They respond punctually to phone calls, are flexible, and meet the requests of the bereaved with generosity. Furthermore, with most civil celebrants anything goes, unlike the clergy, who will be discriminating about what is 'appropriate' in the context of a Christian service without – one hopes – being censorious. Small wonder that the Church of England is feeling the draught.

Christian funerals

Those individuals and families who continue to request a Christian funeral for their loved one, and who look to the Church of England for help, are doing so for a variety of reasons.

- Many are faithful Anglicans and loyal members of our congregations. For them a funeral in church, not just at the

---

6 *Civil Funerals*, Civil Ceremonies Ltd, 2009, © Civil Ceremonies Ltd.

crematorium or cemetery chapel, is a natural and instinctive choice, reflecting both their beliefs and a network of supportive relationships beyond the immediate family.

- For some (including those planning their own funeral in advance), what is uppermost in their thinking is a sense of connection with a place or a community: it is where they feel they *belong*. This is often the case in rural areas where a sense of community is strong. Such sensibility may go hand in hand with religious conviction, but not necessarily so.

- For others the choice of an Anglican funeral is a matter of convention or family tradition. In the past some clergy have been critical of such approaches, but in an era in which familial ties are strained and a sense of belonging fragile, such requests should never be scorned or trivialized. On the contrary, we need to invest in the contacts we have, however tenuous, and build on them. It is crucial to our mission.

- For yet others the request for an Anglican funeral is generated by a connection with a particular church or, more likely, a particular minister. In a society in which the relational is prized above the institutional, we should always welcome such requests and not put unnecessary obstacles in the way. If we handle the approach badly we will simply drive those making it into the open arms of secular celebrants. A funeral director understands the constraints of parish boundaries and the protocols within which most clergy operate, but the bereaved are unlikely to. They are likely to find church structures puzzling and unnecessarily complicated. If there is tension or jealousy among local clergy it is easy for such requests to spark a turf war, accusations of 'pinching funerals' being fired off left, right and centre. Acrimony does not advance the gospel, but where there is trust and collaboration among local ministers, funerals are rarely a contentious issue.

- Then there are those who, although they do not attend church regularly, still see the Church of England as a benign institution to which they are linked – however tenuously – that can bring significance and meaning in the face of death. This is a shrinking constituency, though they may not yet be ready to

tick the box 'no religion' on a census form. We need actively
and generously to engage with these nominal Anglicans and,
above all, meet them where they are in the way that civil celebrants are doing. Unfortunately we are not always operating
on a level playing field. Some funeral directors are antipathetic
to Christianity and will actively steer their clients away from
the church into the arms of a so-called 'non-denominational
minister'. But this should not distract us from the challenge
of pastoral engagement and service.

How we respond to the diverse expectations of this wide-ranging
clientele will determine many people's future attitude to the
Church of England, and by association to all things Christian.
Discernment, having 'a right judgement in all things', is funda-
mental to an effective pastoral ministry. We need to ask ourselves:
'What is right in this context?' One funeral director, speaking of
a priest in his area, commented, 'Father John is always getting
in a muddle. He thinks a wedding is a funeral, and a funeral is a
wedding. He just never pitches it right.' Fine tuning our response
so that we do pitch it right will be the subject of the chapters that
follow.

A funeral can provide a unique opportunity to build bridges
with the local community, many of whom may never have had any
contact with the church – or indeed rebuild bridges where relationships have come under strain. A 'good funeral' is a good advert for
the church. It makes connections with and for people and enables
them to glimpse the resurrected Christ in the midst of their grief.
Sadly the reverse is also true. One poor experience at one funeral
can have a knock-on effect with several families and compound a
sense of alienation. In the increasingly competitive funeral market
we need to lead all funerals as well as possible. We need to raise
our game and be known for the quality with which we conduct
funerals and for the care we extend to the bereaved. Unless we do
so and address the decline in Christian funerals, we are in danger
of ending up in a religious ghetto talking to ourselves.

2

When someone dies

Fear no more the heat o' the sun,
Nor the furious winter's rages;
Thou thy worldly task hast done,
Home art gone, and ta'en thy wages.
Golden lads and girls all must,
As chimney-sweepers, come to dust.

Fear no more the frown o' the great;
Thou art past the tyrant's stroke;
Care no more to clothe and eat;
To thee the reed is as the oak.
The sceptre, learning, physic, must
All follow this, and come to dust.

Fear no more the lightning-flash,
Nor the all-dreaded thunder stone;
Fear not slander, censure rash;
Thou hast finish'd joy and moan.
All lovers young, all lovers must
Consign to thee, and come to dust.

No exorciser harm thee!
Nor no witchcraft charm thee!

Ghost unlaid forbear thee!
Nothing ill come near thee!
Quiet consummation have;
And renowned be thy grave!

William Shakespeare (1564–1616)
from *Cymbeline*

'Death is nothing at all.' These words extracted from a sermon preached in St Paul's Cathedral in 1910 by Henry Scott Holland, so popular at funerals and memorial services, have always sounded a hollow note for me. Far from being nothing at all, death is huge, final, powerful and irrevocable. Even when expected at the end of a long or painful illness, it can still come as a shock. The silence of death has always struck me. After listening to the irregular breathing of the dying, perhaps for hours, or watching the rise and fall of the heart monitor beside a hospital bed, suddenly there is silence and stillness.

It is a privilege to be with someone when they die, but few of us experience it. We lead such busy lives, and with families scattered, time and geography mean that with the best will in the world it is not always possible to be present at the bedside of a dying parent or cherished friend. In earlier generations, when life expectancy was shorter and war and disease a constant reality, death was less remote. Today we like to kid ourselves that we are immortal. Death is often squirrelled away in hospital wards. As a consequence some feel insecure and frightened in the presence of death. We are uncertain what death is, what happens to us when we die or what to do. Busyness can then become an excuse rather than a reason to be absent, so that we do not have to confront our fears.

Most of us, if we have any choice, would prefer to die in our own beds at home surrounded by those whom we love. But it doesn't always work out like that. Many of us die in hospital, and sadly a few die neglected, unnoticed and unloved in an anonymous flat or under a railway arch. One of the huge contributions to modern medicine has been the hospice movement which offers

a quality of holistic care to the terminally ill and their families rarely possible in a busy acute hospital. Domiciliary services provide round-the-clock nursing support, with the result that some patients are never admitted to the hospice at all but are looked after in their own home or that of a relative right to the end. There remain a few diseases for which pain is harder to control and that generate headlines calling for legislation to permit assisted dying, but these are exceptions to the rule. Generally speaking, modern palliative care means that most people die free from pain and distress, and with dignity.

In the Christian tradition, as in most religions, preparing for death and the moment of death itself are events to be enfolded in prayer. Sitting with a terminally ill friend or relative and sharing memories is a profound experience. Christians are familiar with the phrase 'last rites' as shorthand for the ministrations of a priest or minister in the run-up to death. Ideally it is best if the person is still conscious in order to pray with them and perhaps to hear their confession. They may need to unburden themselves of disturbing memories or a troubled conscience, and be assured of God's love and forgiveness. Family and friends may wish to join in receiving Holy Communion with the person. Singing songs and hymns around the bedside or simply reciting the familiar words of the twenty-third psalm can be a wonderful gift to a dying person. In Anglican custom, as in other Christian traditions, the offering of prayer may include anointing the person, making the sign of the cross in oil on their forehead and on the palms of their hands and commending them to the care of their Creator. Touch and hearing being the last of our senses to go, such intimacy can communicate powerfully God's abiding love to a dying person.

Common Worship: Pastoral Services provides a selection of prayers that can be used on these occasions, including the ancient Prayer of Commendation, or a variant of it, which may be said in the hour of death. Addressing the dying person by name, it is a valedictory, commending the person to God the Holy Trinity and in the confidence of Christ's redemption, giving them permission 'to let go' and entrust themselves into God's everlasting arms:

N, go forth upon your journey from this world,
in the name of God the Father almighty who created you:
in the name of Jesus Christ who suffered death for you;
in the name of the Holy Spirit who strengthens you;
in communion with the blessed saints,
and aided by angels and archangels,
and all the armies of the heavenly host.
May your portion this day be in peace,
and your dwelling the heavenly Jerusalem. (p. 229)

Common Worship also provides this prayer:

Gracious God,
nothing in death or life,
nothing in the world as it is,
nothing in the world as it shall be,
nothing in all creation can separate us from your love.
Jesus commended his spirit into your hands at his last hour.
Into those same hands we now commend your servant N,
that dying to the world and cleansed from sin,
death may be for *him/her* the gate to life
and to eternal fellowship with you;
through the same Jesus Christ our Lord. (p. 230)

What happens next?

When someone dies at home, assuming the death is expected, the first thing that a relative needs to do is contact the person's GP to certify the death. It is most likely that the deceased person has been under medical care for some time, so this should be straightforward. If the doctor is satisfied with the cause of death, he or she will issue a Death Certificate, officially entitled the Medical Certificate of Cause of Death. If the person has died in a care home or nursing home, the home's staff usually undertake this duty and liaise again with the deceased person's GP. Similarly, when a person dies in hospital, the hospital staff arrange for the

doctor who was looking after them to issue a certificate. In all cases they must have seen the patient within the last 14 days to be able to issue the certificate. A cremation has to be supported by a second doctor certifying the cause of death and there must be no suspicious circumstances surrounding the death to justify an inquest. Either the hospital staff or the funeral director will advise on this. These additional safeguards are imposed because once a body has been cremated there is no further opportunity to examine the evidence.

When someone dies unexpectedly the process of registration is more complicated. In England and Wales the coroner has to be notified, and in Scotland the procurator fiscal. If the person had not been under medical supervision on a regular basis, then either the GP or out-of-hours doctor, hospital doctor or the police will inform the requisite authority, who may order a post-mortem examination to establish the cause of death. Until this is resolved it will not be possible to finalize the funeral arrangements. Identification of the body of a relative or friend at a morgue is almost always a harrowing experience and, if at all possible, should not be undertaken alone.

Removal of donated organs

The removal of donated organs from a dead body can be a controversial act, even when the deceased carried a Donor Card or signed up on the NHS Donor Register authorizing such an action upon their death. Suddenly all sorts of strange fears and anxieties can surface in the minds of relatives, and need to be addressed. The removal of donated organs following death or the donation of the entire body to a local medical school for medical teaching or research is governed by the provisions of the Anatomy Act (1984) and the Human Tissue Act (2004). Access to corpses in the UK for the use of medical science is regulated by the Human Tissue Authority. Although the deceased will have left a signed document in relation to whole-body donation, a copy of which will also have been lodged with the office of the appointed Licensed Teacher of Anatomy in the medical school, the deceased may not

have informed members of their family of their wishes, and this can create problems. It is not unknown for such donations to be disputed by relatives, either for reasons similar to those for opposing a post-mortem examination or because the funeral in cases of whole-body donation – organized by the medical school – may be delayed for up to two years.

For centuries Christians were concerned about the proper burial of bodies because it was believed that on the Day of Judgement everyone would literally emerge from their graves to meet the Lord. This belief lies behind the traditional custom of burying people with their feet pointing east, so they would be facing in the right direction when Jesus appeared at the Second Coming. With the revival of cremation in the nineteenth century, some Christians recoiled from the idea because they were worried they would not have a body on the Day of Judgement. Similar anxieties can fuel a reluctance to permit organ donation. Today the vast majority of Christians no longer view God's eternal purposes through such literal interpretations of the Bible, any more than they worry about the eternal destiny of those who have been disfigured in accidents or lost limbs in war. God's resurrection power is greater than our limited human understanding. How much less should we worry if we donate our organs in order to help people with debilitating and untreatable illnesses? Nevertheless, half-articulated anxieties do need to be unearthed and addressed.

Caring for the body

The care of the body in death remains a central concern for every family. For centuries, and still in many traditional communities, when a person dies at home the family wash the body and prepare it for burial or cremation themselves, rather than request that this very intimate and personal act be 'undertaken' by someone else. For many people it is the last thing they can do for their loved one. Following death the body remains warm for a couple of hours, but thereafter rigor mortis sets in. Chemical changes in the muscles cause the body to stiffen and it becomes difficult to move or

manipulate. This is why it is important to close the eyelids and mouth, and to straighten the limbs as far as possible. Before wrapping the body in a clean sheet or clean clothes as preferred, it is usually advisable to tie the ankles together with a bandage, and fold the arms across the chest. This makes it easier to move the body. The phrase 'dead weight' is not without meaning!

When a death occurs at home, things tend to happen fast. It is important, therefore, that a family does not feel rushed so that they lose control of the situation. Even if a family does not wish to be involved in the preparation of the body for burial or cremation, they may value just sitting with the body of their loved one to think and pray or reminisce for a couple of hours before it is removed from the home. I remember when my maternal grandmother, aged 94, died at home. The doctor, who had been summoned earlier that morning, arrived within ten minutes of her death. He advised my mother to phone the undertakers, who arrived 20 minutes later. In the space of just half an hour my grandmother's body had been removed from the house, leaving an empty bed and my mother alone, dazed by the pace of events.

Saying prayers with a grieving family around the body of a loved one is a special moment as they come to terms with what has happened, and it should not be hurried. If the clergy know the family and have accompanied the elderly or sick person in their last days, it is good to open up a conversation with the relatives in advance of death so that they can think how they want to handle things when the inevitable finally happens.

Registering the death

In most cases it is the next of kin or close relative who goes to register the death. Contact details for the registrar, including opening times of the office, are available from the local council. The registrar will require the following information:

- Full name of the deceased
- Date and place of birth

- Date and place of death
- Occupation of deceased
- Address
- If the deceased was in receipt of a pension or allowance from public funds
- The date of birth of the surviving spouse/civil partner (if applicable)

The registrar will also require the following documents:

- Deceased's Birth Certificate
- Medical Certificate of Cause of Death (Death Certificate)
- Deceased's National Health Service Medical Card (if available)
- Deceased's Marriage/Civil Partnership Certificate (if applicable)

The registrar (in England and Wales) will then register the death and issue a green Certificate of Disposal giving permission for the burial or cremation to proceed. In Scotland a white certificate is issued by the procurator fiscal. This certificate will be needed by the funeral director before the funeral can take place. If the coroner has been notified of the death and decides that a post-mortem is necessary, burial or cremation will be delayed until that has been done. If the post-mortem shows that the death was from natural causes and there is to be a burial, the coroner will issue a certificate to the registrar who will then register the death and issue the green certificate for disposal. If there is to be a cremation the coroner will issue a yellow form authorizing it.

If the post-mortem does not show that the death was from natural causes, the coroner will start an investigation, which may include an inquest. In such cases it will be the coroner who will issue a certificate authorizing burial or a yellow form authorizing cremation, together with interim certificates of the fact of death to facilitate the administration of the deceased's affairs. If there is an inquest, the death cannot be registered until the coroner

has issued a certificate, which will happen afterwards. Once the death is registered, certified copies of the Death Certificate can be obtained either at the time of the registration of death or subsequently if required for tax or legal purposes. An additional fee will be charged by the registrar.

The will

If the deceased person made a will, it is likely that they will have recorded their wishes in respect of the type of funeral they want, including whether they wish to be buried or cremated. They may also have stipulated where they wish to be buried or be cremated. A will should be kept in a safe and secure place. Some people deposit it with their bank or solicitor, but this isn't always the case. The executor or at least a member of the family or a close friend should know where it is kept. If it cannot be located, and if a solicitor drew up the will, then he or she is likely to have a copy. It is important to consult the will *before* finalizing the funeral arrangements. In many parishes it is not unusual for members of the congregation to discuss their funeral wishes with their parish priest and to deposit written instructions with him or her in advance of the event. If this is done, it is sensible to advise the parishioner concerned also to give a copy of their instructions to their next of kin so that there are no surprises or disagreements when arrangements have to be made.

The estate

When someone dies, a Grant of Representation is normally required, unless the estate is small – generally less than £5,000 – and does not include things like land and property, stocks and shares or some insurance policies. If the deceased left a will, the executor(s) must obtain a Grant of Probate from the court before the deceased's property and possessions can be distributed in accordance with their wishes, and any outstanding debts and

liabilities are paid. This can be a difficult and time-consuming process. Where there is no will and the person is deemed to have died 'intestate', it will usually be the nearest family member who will obtain Letters of Administration from the court before the deceased's property and possessions can be distributed according to law. The person who obtains Letters of Administration is called the administrator. In Scotland the term used for a Grant of Representation is Confirmation. Different procedures exist in Northern Ireland and in the Republic of Ireland.

Suicide

The unexpected death of a person is always a shock, but when they have taken their own life the resulting trauma for friends and family is enormous. Sometimes, when for example a person has had a long history of mental illness, a suicide is likely to be coped with more easily by those left behind than when it has seemingly come out of the blue. The suicide of a young person is a particular tragedy. A bereaved family will have all the usual feelings of grief to cope with, but their grief will be shot through with disbelief, puzzlement and – in all probability – considerable anger. Sometimes a person leaves a suicide note to explain their course of action, but not always. Conversations among friends and relatives as they attempt to come to terms with what has happened will be punctuated with questions and regrets. There will be many 'whys', 'what ifs' and 'if onlys' to deal with, none of which are ever likely to receive a satisfactory answer.[1] Counsellors like to talk about 'closure'. With a suicide there is rarely closure for those left behind.

Common Worship provides these two sensitive prayers after a suicide:[2]

---

1 See Appendix E, 'After a suicide', p. 158.
2 *Common Worship: Pastoral Services* (2000), London: CHP, p. 360.

Eternal God and Father,
look in mercy on those who remember N before you.
Let not the manner of *his/her* death
cloud the good memories of *his/her* life.
For N the trials of this world are over
and death is past.
Accept from us all that we feel
even when words fail;
deliver us from despair
and give us strength to meet the days to come
in the faith of Jesus Christ our Lord. **Amen.**

God our strength and our redeemer:
you do not leave us in this life
nor abandon us in death.
Hear our prayer for those in despair,
when days are full of darkness
and the future empty of hope.
Renew in them your sustaining strength
for we believe that there is nothing in all creation
that can separate us from your love
in Christ Jesus our Lord. **Amen.**

Attendant upon so many unanswered questions invariably erupts
a tide of remorse and guilt. People revisit the past and scrutinize
the behaviour of the deceased, looking for clues that might offer
some insight into the circumstances of the suicide. They yearn to
turn the clock back and in their imaginations construct different
scenarios with different outcomes. Anger may be directed towards
the person who committed suicide, but equally may be directed
towards other members of the family or mutual friends, work colleagues, the medical profession or indeed towards themselves for
failing to intervene or spot the seriousness of the situation. And
mingled with the anger there will be guilt and shame, particularly
if the death provoked unhelpful publicity.

Sometimes what emerges in the wake of a suicide are disturbing
revelations about the person who died, including events that may

have pushed them over the edge. Depression, hidden addictions, undisclosed relationships or affairs and mounting debts are common factors in suicide. Presiding at the funeral of someone who has taken their own life in such circumstances requires extraordinary sensitivity because there is so much raw emotion to handle. Until relatively recently it was forbidden to bury suicides in consecrated ground. At the commencement of the Order for the Burial of the Dead in the Book of Common Prayer, it explicitly states: 'Here it is to be noted, that the Office ensuing is not to be used for any that die unbaptized, or excommunicate, or have laid violent hands upon themselves.' This rubric was inserted under pressure from Puritan divines at the Savoy Conference in 1661, which had been summoned to discuss revisions to the Prayer Book. In the context of seventeenth-century polity, this all-encompassing rubric prohibited the exercise of the ministrations of the Church to any who were not considered Christian. Interestingly, the *Sunday Services of Methodists with Other Occasional Services*, which was published a century later in 1786 and contained a shortened form of the Anglican burial service, omitted the rubric.

With the passage of the years the blanket prohibition upon Anglican ministers burying suicides has gone, not least because, as Canon lawyers point out, Canon B38, para. 2 (see Appendix A), which governs the interpretation of the rubric, emphasizes that the exclusion applies only when the deceased was 'of sound mind'.[3] Psychologists have garnered various insights into what happens when the human mind is disturbed or depressed, and how a lack of inner equilibrium can distort judgement. For this reason the state has decriminalized suicide. Coroners regularly give the verdict 'while the balance of his/her mind was disturbed'. But shame, in combination with uncertainty about how a given minister may respond to a request from a grieving family for help, still lingers on and is likely to be an added burden the bereaved carry.

If assisted suicide does eventually become law and the verdicts of coroners change, then either the bishops or General Synod will

---

3 Rupert D. H. Bursell (1996), *Liturgy, Order and the Law*, Oxford: Clarendon, pp. 212–13.

need to draft a pastoral variation of the rites as already provided in the Canon. The Church rightly teaches that all life comes from God and that the gift of life is not ours to dispose of. But it also teaches that the eternal God is our refuge and 'underneath are the everlasting arms' (Deut. 33.27). The Church should be at the vanguard of offering a compassionate response in cases of suicide, not compounding tragedy with rejection.

Stillbirths

A stillbirth is one of the most harrowing experiences parents may have to endure. The prospect of the birth of a child generates huge excitement in friends and relatives alike. A baby is expected, but a dead one is born. The birth should have been a time of joy and celebration. In the event it is a time of grief and loss. In past generations, when infant mortality was high, this sort of event may have been sad but was unremarkable and probably glossed over, no doubt at considerable cost to the parents. Legally, because the child was stillborn there was no Birth Certificate, and where no Birth Certificate existed no death could be registered, with the result that most stillbirths were automatically disposed of in hospital incinerators without ceremony. Things have changed. Today the importance of marking the life of the baby in the mother's womb and its premature death is recognized. The grieving father and mother need to acknowledge their parentage and mourn their loss, not least because unacknowledged grief can overwhelm and distort the upbringing of any subsequent children born to them. Legally, although the usual Death Certificate is not issued, the registrar (or coroner) still has to issue a certificate (or order) before burial may take place.[4]

The term 'stillbirth' or 'stillborn' is normally applied to the death of children in the womb after the stage of viability has been reached. If the child was born near to term or at full term, most hospitals will permit parents to spend time with their dead baby

---

4 Bursell, *Liturgy, Order and the Law*, p. 207.

if they want to. Hospital chaplains are adept at being alongside parents in their grief while they decide whether or not they want a funeral for their baby. Most parents will want to name their child. It is always important for a minister to use the correct name of the deceased at a funeral, and in these contexts naming the child frequently in the context of prayer is a real consolation to parents. *Common Worship: Pastoral Services* provides a helpful 'theological note' reflecting on issues surrounding the funerals of children dying near the time of birth,[5] as well as various resources from which a minister can construct a suitable liturgy. Among them is included this prayer for the bereaved family:

> God our creator,
> from whom all life comes,
> comfort this family,
> grieving for the loss of their hoped-for child.
> Help them to find assurance
> that with you nothing is wasted or incomplete,
> and uphold them with your love,
> through Jesus Christ our Saviour. (p. 310)

---

5 *Common Worship: Pastoral Services*, pp. 316–17.

3

The funeral director

The only people who ring before 9 o'clock in the morning are undertakers or bishops.

Jeremy Fletcher, *Rules for Reverends*[1]

Whether clergy like it or not, funeral directors will continue to be the first port-of-call for the bereaved. Gone are the days when the first phone call a bereaved family made was to the parish priest. Some clergy resent this change, feeling that their role is being usurped, but priestly grumpiness merely confirms in many people's minds the arrogance of the Church. Clergy need to get real. Funeral directors are the gatekeepers of funerals and we need them on our side.

In the same way that clergy like to talk about 'baptisms' but people in general talk about 'christenings', so ministers habitually talk about 'undertakers' whereas undertakers prefer to call themselves 'funeral directors'. The old label may still have mileage in rural areas where an undertaker may double-up as a cabinetmaker, joiner or farmer, but in cities and towns the title 'funeral director' is now the norm. It is certainly how they are listed in trade directories and on the internet. The change in title is more than cosmetic. It is indicative both of the professionalization of the role and of the way certain tasks, which in earlier generations were dispersed among a network of relatives and people in the local community, are now regularly subsumed by this all-encompassing manager of death. Funeral directors these days do much more than provide a coffin and transport to and from the crematorium or cemetery. They oversee the whole process of death from the

---

1 Jeremy Fletcher (2013), *Rules for Reverends*, Abingdon: BRF, p. 11.

mortuary to the grave and, as we have noted, it is not unknown for them to preside at a funeral ceremony itself.

Observers of this quiet evolution point to the way North American funeral customs continue to reshape the British scene. For example, many funeral directors now describe their premises as 'funeral homes'. In pursuit of greater choice, the great mantra of twenty-first-century society, some commentators predict that it won't be long before chapels of rest are enlarged and equipped with lecterns and sound systems so that funeral services can be offered from funeral homes. This is already happening in some areas in the UK. Why bother to go to a cold draughty church when something altogether more modern and comfortable is available all in one?

In these developments cynics see further evidence of the commercialization of death akin to that famously exposed by Jessica Mitford in her book, *The American Way of Death*.[2] But it does create problems, at least for Anglican ministers. Under the Burial Act (1880) it is illegal for a Church of England minister to conduct a funeral service in a funeral director's private chapel. This prohibition was restated in Canon B38 para. 1 in 1987 and revised in 2003. Some clergy and funeral directors quietly ignore the prohibition, but if this development continues there will need to be a reappraisal of the situation with consequent revision of the Canon.

Part of the trouble is that most clergy perceive themselves to be the 'funeral director' and resent the encroachment of undertakers on their sacred territory. This underlying tension can erupt into open conflict when relationships are fraught. If this happens it is both sad and bad, and certainly inappropriate if it impacts on a

---

2 In *The American Way of Death*, first published in 1963, Jessica Mitford castigates abuses associated with the funeral-home industry in North America. Mitford was highly critical of its commercialization and controversially exposed ways some funeral directors take advantage of the shock and grief of the bereaved to convince them to pay far more than necessary for a funeral and other services. An updated revision, *The American Way of Death Revisited*, was completed by her shortly before her death in 1996, and published in 1998.

grieving family. Given that funeral directors have the body (and possession is nine-tenths of the law), clergy would do better to build strong and positive relationships with funeral directors and stop bemoaning their fate. Collaboration is the name of the game in funerals as in other forms of ministry.

Today in the UK over half of registered funeral directors belong either to Co-operative Funeralcare or to the Dignity Group. The Co-op boasts a network of over 850 funeral homes and carries out around 100,000 funerals a year. According to its website, Dignity operates a network of over 1,000 funeral directors, with local firms either owned or approved by Dignity. The group carries out over 62,000 funerals a year. In recent years Dignity has further diversified. In part as a result of cutbacks in local government budgets, they now also own or manage a number of crematoria and cemeteries. The remainder of funerals in the UK are conducted either by localized groups of funeral directors, often owned by a management company, or by independent funeral directors, the majority of whom are small, family-run businesses. Some of these businesses may have been in a family for three or four generations. Independent funeral directors particularly value their partnership with the local clergy.

Most funeral directors these days offer pre-paid funeral plans. Rather like taking out life insurance or writing a will, it enables a person to put their affairs in good order before they die. This safeguards their next of kin and executors from much of the hassle, and usually sets out in some detail the deceased's wishes. It also protects a family from rising costs, at least in theory.

Like the clergy, and indeed other professions, funeral directors come in all shapes and sizes. There will always be the occasional bad apple, but most are conscientious, caring individuals; some are outstanding in the service they offer their clients. Obviously funeral directors are running a business and need to earn a living, so it would be naive not to acknowledge a degree of self-interest even in the best of them. That said, most take their work seriously and are scrupulous in their dealings. They are there to help a family through a difficult time and have a real concern for their clients. Some see it not just as a service to the public but as a

vocation. Clergy should never think that they have a monopoly on pastoral care.

How do funeral directors rate the clergy?

Research conducted by the University of Chester[3] into funerals in the Warrington area interviewed clergy, local funeral directors and the bereaved both before and after a funeral to ascertain and evaluate their experience. The results matched anecdotal findings gleaned from a series of meetings with undertakers in Cheshire and south Manchester over a six-month period. The general tone of the feedback on Anglican funerals was very positive. Funeral directors reported enjoying good working relationships with the vast majority of clergy and felt that most of the time the Church of England is doing a good job for the bereaved. In their perception, what distinguishes Anglican funerals from those conducted by secular, humanist or civil celebrants are principally three things:

- **Realism**
  The Christian approach to death is distinctive because it is shaped by a belief in the transformative power of the resurrection of Jesus Christ. In presiding over 'life-centred' commemorations, civil celebrants are sometimes weak at facing the reality of death or its tragedy. Somewhat bizarrely, in secular funerals death can be 'the elephant in the room'.

- **Hope**
  The Christian minister offers hope, not just empathy. Hope is the underrated virtue of St Paul's famous trinity of faith,

---

3 In 2012 the Church of England Deanery of Great Budworth in the Diocese of Chester and Deanery of Warrington in the Diocese of Liverpool formed a Promoting Anglican Funerals group (PAF), which subsequently collaborated with the University of Chester Department of Media to survey attitudes about Anglican funerals and to suggest means by which mission and ministry can be supported to increase the number of Anglican funerals in the area.

hope and love. It runs deeper than glib optimism because it is rooted in the God who brings good out of evil and light out of darkness. And as Paul says, 'hope does not disappoint us' (Rom. 5.5). By contrast, funeral directors say how 'bleak' humanist funerals can be. Paradoxically, in an age in which hymn singing has gone out of fashion, they also report that what congregations at secular or humanist funerals often miss is singing a hymn!

- **Pastoral care**
  The involvement of a humanist or civil celebrant with a bereaved family finishes at the crematorium or cemetery gate. A Christian funeral is not an employment contract. A Christian minister is committed to the ongoing pastoral care of the bereaved in the months that follow. In the words of one priest, 'We're here for the whole journey.' The challenge for the church community is to be true to that vision and make it a reality.

Funeral directors also report that the Church of England is at its best when handling tragedy. When a death has affected an entire community, where feelings are raw and emotions are running high, or where there has been a fallout in a family, the formality of an Anglican funeral can be immensely reassuring. It offers a strong structure to hold a grieving congregation secure. The liturgy creates conduits to channel the tide of raw emotions safely.

Room for improvement

Against this positive backcloth, funeral directors register some gripes and irritations. There was the occasional horror story of clergy getting the name of the deceased wrong or turning up at a crematorium looking a mess, wearing trainers and a surplice that had seen better days. The report of one priest turning up late for a funeral wearing jeans and a T-shirt and, standing next to

the coffin and within earshot of the family, saying to the under-taker, 'Right, what have we got here then?' was painful to hear. By and large, however, research reveals that Anglican ministers do a really good job. Clergy need to hear that vote of confidence and be reassured by it. But there is always room for improvement, specifically in the following areas:

- **Communication**
  A frequent complaint of funeral directors is that the clergy, unlike their secular competitors, are slow to agree to conduct a funeral, often leaving a grieving family uncertain about the arrangements or missing a deadline for a death notice in the local paper. In terms of responding to phone calls, one funeral director said that the same day is ideal, but the next day is acceptable. When clergy do not return phone calls promptly or within 24 hours, or sometimes not at all, funeral directors will look elsewhere. Sometimes they find themselves trawling through lists of retired clergy in a desperate attempt to find a minister at short notice. To get round this problem, some parishes purchase a dedicated church mobile phone, which is then held by a rota of trusted church people who take calls from funeral directors and themselves make the necessary arrangements for the funeral.

- **Attitude**
  Although the Church of England has a duty of care to every-one in the nation, some clergy will only conduct the funerals of known members of their congregations. This is in contra-vention of the Canons of the Church of England which state that, 'It is the duty of every parochial minister to officiate at the funerals or interment of those who die within their cure, or any parishioner or persons whose names are entered on the church electoral roll of the parish whether deceased within his cure or elsewhere' (Canon B38). This may be the letter of the law, but it is impossible to police the situation. In the rueful words of one funeral director, 'There are clergy who serve the public, and those who think the public serves them.'

- **Holidays and days off**

No one is available 24 hours a day, 365 days a year. We all need to rest and to switch off. Good pastoral care takes a lot of energy, and uninterrupted time off is essential to resource funeral ministry. But how do we field pastoral emergencies and ensure that funeral enquiries are dealt with courteously and promptly? Funeral directors sometimes joke about clergy and their 'days off'. 'Nobody begrudges them holidays and time off, but why does "day off" translate as "uncontactable"?' asked one undertaker.

A particular problem is Fridays. Many stipendiary clergy like to have Friday as their day off, which is fine except that it means there are fewer clergy available to cover funerals on that day. What complicates matters is that Friday is increasing in popularity as a day for funerals among clients in full-time employment. They often opt for Friday because that way they can recover over the weekend without having to take additional time off work. Ministers do need to sort out locally or on a deanery basis how best to cover for one another on days off and during holidays, and to let the local funeral directors know their arrangements, preferably by email, providing them with accurate contact details.[4] This is particularly important where clergy are not supported by a parish office or an administrator. If we don't do this, we should not moan when funeral directors look elsewhere for officiants.

- **Impersonal and inflexible**

In company with feedback from some bereaved families, the most serious criticism levelled against the Church of England by funeral directors is that we often come across as old-fashioned, tired, inflexible and stuffy. One funeral director

---

4 A good example of this is the Chilterns Chaplaincy Service, where ministers have collaborated to form a rota for local funeral directors, with two ministers always on call each day to cover funerals at the local cemeteries or crematoria.

said that he had one retired clergyman in his patch who insisted on having 'Thine be the Glory' at the end of every funeral no matter what the family said. Another funeral director said that when he had a 'difficult funeral' he always went to the United Reformed Church or to the local Methodist minister because they were much more flexible than the Church of England.

It is evident that the funerals conducted by – admittedly – a minority of clergy are still woefully *impersonal*. Things have improved considerably since the bad old days of the 'duty minister at the crem', who might have been conducting six or seven cremations that day and was unlikely to have known the deceased or to have met the family until they got out of the funeral cars and walked into the crematorium chapel. Small wonder that he – and it would have been a 'he' in those days – rarely said anything personal about the deceased and could appear remote. Those days have largely gone, but sadly it appears that some ministers are still referring to the deceased as 'our dear brother/sister departed' and never mention the person's name. Although a small minority, such ministers fuel the Church's reputation for cold formality. Things are not helped by 'crem cowboys' – ministers, lay or ordained, who hang around crematoria taking funerals for just about anybody. Thankfully there are few of them, but they damage the Church's reputation.

In an age where the relational and informality are paramount, too many clergy and Readers are not connecting with people, particularly younger people. Classic symptoms are lack of warmth, a mechanistic use of set prayers, not looking at the congregation, not mentioning any personal details and never observing any pauses for reflection, so that a funeral is all over in 15 minutes.

- **Professionalism**
Funeral directors bemoan the poor dress-sense of some ministers. 'If we turned up at a funeral the way some of the clergy do, we'd be out of a job', is not an uncommon complaint.

Appearance matters. Looking a mess does not communicate competence or professionalism, and it undermines the confidence of both funeral directors and families in the minister. Funeral directors also record frustration at a minority of clergy who still refuse to use email.

- **Readers and retired clergy**
  With the reduction in stipendiary clergy, many deaneries are dependent on the services of Readers and retired clergy not simply on Sundays but for taking funerals midweek. Most do a wonderful job, but it is also clear that some elderly Readers and retired clergy can become confused and inaudible when conducting funerals. It is the job of an incumbent to ensure that their Readers and assistant clergy offer a reasonable standard of ministry, and they would be wise to monitor discreetly their funerals from time to time.

Funeral directors insist that the Church must change and adapt or the growth in secular funerals will continue unabated. The day when parsons simply offered a 'traditional funeral' is over. The reluctance of the Church of England to participate fully in the National Funeral Exhibition, which happens every other year, is an embarrassment and is indicative of how remote we have become from the fast-evolving landscape of death in this country.

Fees

The Church of England, along with other denominations, operates strict protocols in relation to fees, which since 2013 are legally the property of the Boards of Finance of dioceses, not of individual ministers, be they lay or ordained. Individual dioceses may operate differing arrangements within the national parameters for retired clergy, self-supporting ministers, OLMs, house-for-duty clergy and Readers. But by and large the new regime has introduced welcome clarity into an area that had been somewhat murky and on occasion open to abuse.

In spite of the new guidelines, some funeral directors continue to level criticism at clergy and parishes about their lack of transparency in handling fees. Some clergy charge unjustifiable travel expenses. A frequent lack of invoices and receipts is another recurrent frustration, leaving a firm potentially exposed if a client questions their scale of charges. Like funeral directors, parishes and ministers need to protect themselves by keeping up-to-date records of funerals and of all monies received or passed on. Then, if there is a complaint or investigation, they can point to a paper-trail or their email record of what was agreed and what transpired. It is all about accountability and integrity.

The way funeral fees are collected within the new statutory framework will vary from diocese to diocese. Poor inner-city parishes and some rural parishes may feel challenged by the need to adapt and crank up their financial and administrative systems, including, where necessary, getting to grips with online banking. Some may need diocesan support to do this. Collectively, however, the Church needs to bring its systems up to speed and embody good practice in relation to fees, as follows:

1 A funeral booking is received from a funeral director and is acknowledged by phone promptly.
2 Email confirmation is received from the funeral director.
3 Email invoice sent ahead of the funeral by the parish or minister to the funeral director.
4 A funeral director should pay one cheque to the PCC for the total cost of a funeral, including the organist and verger. Alternatively, there could be a BACS payment into the parish account. Whichever system is preferred, there should be no cash payments and no money should be paid into the accounts of ministers.
5 A receipt for the BACS payment is sent by email.
6 Payments to retired ministers, organists, musicians, vergers and so on by the local church should be in accordance with diocesan policy and either by cheque or by BACS, but *never cash*.

Funeral directors and the bereaved

A decade ago a funeral director may have been able to advise a bereaved family about a funeral. This still happens and much will depend on context, but these days it is not unusual for relatives, particularly from middle-class families, to arrive at the undertakers in the High Street armed with a list of requirements. Families have often researched funerals online before meeting with the funeral director. They may also have noted aspects of funerals they have attended recently or seen in a film or on television; they then come to the funeral director with specific ideas about the funeral they are arranging. Such things place new demands on funeral directors, which in turn can translate into points of tension between funeral directors and clergy as they negotiate the shape of a service on behalf of the family.

Funeral directors rightly see it as their job to listen carefully to a family's needs and respond to their choices. If families request a civil celebrant, it is their job to provide one. Funeral directors are not naive, and some talk of individual civil celebrants in their areas actively touting for work. They say that although the Church often offers better and cheaper funerals, they have a professional duty to ascertain the choice of each family and respond accordingly.

Of course, as in all conversations, the way questions are asked invariably dictates the answer we get. 'Are you religious?' is a classic example. To such a question put by a funeral director, many British people today will answer 'No'. The words 'religion' and 'religious' have acquired a negative connotation in many circles. There is a wariness and antipathy towards faith, fuelled by an underlying assumption that religion is the partner of arrogance and intolerance. The facts do not support the stigmatization, but there is no escaping the way Christianity is regularly pilloried in some quarters. In the current climate few British people will respond positively to a question about religious commitment from a funeral director. A hesitant or negative reply may mean no more than they do not go to church regularly, but they would still want to have a Christian service that included a couple of hymns and the Lord's Prayer. An ambivalent response, however, may encourage some funeral directors,

particularly if they have no faith themselves, to suggest that they opt for a funeral conducted by a civil celebrant, whereas a generation ago it would have been the local vicar who was automatically contacted. Another classic question asked by funeral directors is, 'Do you have your own minister?' Again the answer from many people is likely to be 'No'. 'Would you like me to find a minister for you?' 'Yes please', replies the grateful client. Once again, some funeral directors may choose to interpret this as an invitation to approach a civil funeral celebrant or non-denominational minister of his/her own choice.

Everyone involved in funeral ministry, in whatever capacity, constantly needs to remind themselves just how vulnerable the bereaved can be. Although the law presents a narrow definition of what it means to be a 'vulnerable adult', the Church in particular should be more generous than the statutory definition, the better to reflect the integrity of pastoral care and the ethics of compassion that lie at the heart of the Christian gospel. In all meetings with the bereaved it is important to maintain professional boundaries, not least because of the intimacy death opens up.[5] This vigilance is as vital for funeral directors as for ministers, counsellors and bereavement visitors, not least because a bereaved family is likely to be in shock when they first meet the undertaker. Funeral directors have enormous power and they need to be scrupulous in how they present various options to grieving relatives – from the type of coffin to be used, whether the funeral is to be followed by burial or cremation, to the place and character of the funeral service. Pressure of time may mean that both parties are concerned to get the arrangements finalized there and then, particularly if relatives live a long way away.

Investing in a professional partnership

The vast majority of funeral directors seek to build professional and friendly relationships with the clergy with whom they work. But just as clergy have opinions about their local undertakers, so

5 See *Guidelines for the Professional Conduct of the Clergy*, London: CHP, 2003 (in the process of being revised).

funeral directors discuss their experience of the clergy and churches and compare notes. They know who is reliable, who 'does a good funeral', who is unpunctual and who is downright unco-operative or rude. Many funeral directors keep a list of the 'dos' and don'ts' of each minister and of the various churches with which they work regularly. It was the observation of some funeral directors that older clergy tend to be less flexible in their approach.

A regular charm offensive with local funeral directors, dropping by for a chat over a cup of coffee, exercising genuine pastoral care of them, respecting and supporting them in their work with the bereaved, will do more good than clerical criticism. To put it bluntly, *there are few better ways of arresting the decline in church funerals and ensuring that funerals are not directed elsewhere than by making friends with the local funeral directors*. Clergy need to be professional in their dealings with funeral directors, but even more they need to demonstrate that they are interested in them as people and not merely as business partners. Churches and ministers need to model best practice:

- Return the phone calls of funeral directors punctually and courteously.
- Contact the bereaved straight away to assure them that you are on the case, even if it is just to leave a message and say you will be in touch again soon. Do not leave things until the last minute.
- Listen to what the family would like. Do not presume you know best.
- Phone the local funeral directors on a Monday to see if anyone has died over the weekend. Don't always wait for them to contact you.
- If your parish has an electronic diary, share it online with the local funeral directors so they can see at a glance when the church might be free for a funeral.
- Give funeral directors ample notice of holidays.
- Provide them with the contact details of those covering for absence, including days off.

4

The bereaved

I was crying on the inside of my face, only you didn't notice.

A bereaved parishioner

The bereaved seek comfort and help in their hour of need but invariably bring a clutch of inchoate beliefs, often with little or no Christian background to shape them. Clergy are familiar with funerals, crematoria and cemeteries but can easily forget that for most people a funeral is an occasional event. They also forget how incredibly intimidating clergy can be. Uncertainty about procedure and nervousness of the clergy are amplified in bereavement. Some families feel less intimidated by the prospect of a civil celebrant conducting their relative's funeral than the vicar. Although a complete stranger, a civil celebrant may still be less scary than a priest.

Those who do turn to the Church for advice and guidance in their loss value the presence of a minister alongside them in their grief, but they will be acutely sensitive to being patronized, bullied or judged, particularly if their domestic situation or family relationships are complicated. As with weddings, research confirms that it is the quality of the relationship with the officiating minister that counts, and the initial encounter between the minister and the bereaved invariably sets the tone for what follows. Even the voice of the recorded message on the vicarage or parish office answerphone is important because, for the bereaved, at that moment it is the voice of the Church speaking.

The importance of returning the calls of funeral directors promptly and courteously has been stressed. It is not unusual for an undertaker to have a bereaved relative anxiously sitting on the other side of the desk in the office as he or she phones around, trying

to track down a minister and match their availability to vacant slots at the local crematorium. Most crematoria charge different rates for services at different times of the day, the middle of the day typically being the most expensive. Each crematorium will have its own policy about accepting bookings. Some may hold a provisional booking for (say) 48 hours, after which it lapses if it is not confirmed – much to the fury of a family. So it is incumbent upon clergy, lay ministers and parish administrators to co-operate gladly. Given the pressure on funeral directors in some towns, it is perhaps inevitable – though regrettable – when they present clergy with a fait accompli. 'This is the date and the time of the funeral: can you do it?'

It is important that the minister or parish administrator maintain a comprehensive record of every funeral undertaken, both in church and at the local cemetery or crematorium. The name and address of the deceased; the date, time and place of the funeral; the identity of the funeral director all need to be logged. The contact details of the next of kin need to be recorded so that they can be followed up after the funeral to see how they are coping. It is also sensible to record the choice of readings, music and hymns, which organist is booked and whether a verger is scheduled to be in attendance. How much they are paid should also be logged for accounting purposes. If there is to be a retiring collection, this too needs to be noted (see p. 63).

With such a comprehensive record to hand, if for any reason the agreed minister is unavailable or taken ill, someone can easily pick up the baton at short notice and take the funeral. Equally importantly, in the case of any complaint it means that there is a note of who did what. An example of such a funeral record is provided in Appendix B.

Meeting the family

If funeral directors deserve a speedy response to their enquiries, so does a bereaved family. One of the justifiable complaints of funeral directors about a small number of clergy is that they fail

to contact a bereaved family until late on in the process, and a few clergy not at all. Admittedly, for clergy, taking a funeral is just one part of a busy ministry. With a crowded diary they can find themselves juggling funerals alongside school assemblies, sermon preparation, hospital visiting, PCC meetings, midweek Communions and a host of other things. But there is still no excuse for not picking up the phone and making contact with the bereaved, even if it is only to arrange a time later in the day or week to have a fuller conversation. The bereaved seek reassurance. They need to talk, though they may be frightened of anything 'heavy'. Even if they can't see the minister in person they will value hearing the person's voice, not least because with families being widely dispersed, a meeting between the minister and the relatives prior to a funeral is not always practicable. Next of kin may live some distance away and may not be returning to the area until the day of the funeral itself. This is unfortunate, if sometimes unavoidable, but some sort of personal contact is still vital, even if funeral arrangements and personal details about the deceased have to be discussed entirely over the phone or via Skype.

Some clergy are notoriously overbearing and bossy but so are some funeral directors, who may equally try to impose their ideas on a reluctant family and take it upon themselves to decree what will happen, including the choice of hymns. Others may insist that they provide the pall-bearers for the coffin whereas a family may wish to carry their relative's coffin themselves. Provided the proposed family bearers are fit and strong, and of roughly commensurate height, there is nothing wrong with this. After all, it is what happened for centuries and it helps bond a family together in their grief. The very children and grandchildren, who as infants were carried by their dead mother or father, now return the compliment and carry them for the last time. Some funeral directors feel they are the 'professionals' and don't want any emotional amateurs involved. As a result it is not unknown for clergy to find themselves piggy-in-the-middle, being advocates for a distressed family on the one hand and trying to explain the funeral director's concerns to disgruntled relatives on the other.

When meeting a bereaved family and planning the funeral it is important to find out how many mourners they think will be attending the service and who will be present. The dynamics of a big funeral with a packed church or crematorium chapel are very different from a small gathering of a dozen or so mourners. The anticipated size of a congregation will help guide the minister in working out what will and what won't work musically at the funeral. It is particularly important to be alert to any hidden agenda. Increasingly family relationships are complicated and it is not unusual for ex-partners to reappear at a funeral or for estranged siblings to squabble over who sits where or who should walk directly behind the coffin. Such occasions are embarrassing and stressful, not least for the clergy officiating, but they cannot be ignored. If during conversations with a bereaved family it emerges that there is unresolved tension among family members, it is wise to negotiate a seating plan for the church or crematorium chapel in advance to mitigate the chances of open confrontation.

It is also wise, if time permits, to check for a mismatch between how the locals view the deceased and how the family sees things. The locals may have seen dear old Flo as a gentle angel who lived round the corner, minding her own business, whereas the family may have known her as a controlling tyrant. Clergy tend to meet only the family and form a picture based on what they say, whereas workmates or a fellow drinker down the pub may provide a fuller picture of the person.

Viewing the body

For friends and members of the family who have not seen the deceased for a long time, or when the death was unexpected, viewing the body can be a valuable part of the bereavement process. Most but not all funeral directors have a chapel of rest where such viewings can take place in private, and a family may ask the minister to accompany them on such a visit. In recent years a new breed of cut-price funeral directors has emerged offering a 'no frills service'. They reduce their overheads by having no shops in the High

Street and usually advertise their services in local newspapers or on the web. Typically they own neither hearse nor fleet of cars, but hire them as necessary. By law all premises are inspected regularly by local authorities to ensure refrigeration facilities are up to standard, but the premises of cut-price funeral directors tend to be warehouses on small industrial estates. In theory a bereaved family knows all this when they make a booking and are content *not* to see the body of their loved one. But it is not unknown for relatives to change their mind, which can cause problems. Once again clergy can find themselves dragged into a row between client and undertaker in an effort to effect some sort of compromise.

It is rare these days for people to have seen or touched a dead body, and it is wise when escorting a family to a chapel of rest to enquire whether or not any of them have seen a dead person before. If not, the minister would do well to explain what to expect, namely that the face is likely to have a waxen look, be drained of colour, and that the body will be cold. The coldness of a dead body invariably comes as a shock to people. Intellectually they know the person is dead, but at an instinctive level they may still expect the body to be warm, perhaps because the person looks as if they are sleeping.

If there has been a post-mortem, it is important to check with the undertaker the state of the body *before* entering the chapel of rest. Few people realize how invasive an autopsy is and that a body is only roughly stitched back together afterwards. In such circumstances it is imperative that grieving relatives do not become over demonstrative in touching the corpse and end up distressed when they discover the degree of mutilation to it.

For these reasons some morticians apply make-up to a corpse. If the person died in a car accident and there has been considerable trauma to the body, or if, following a post-mortem, the body has badly discoloured, the discreet use of cosmetics can be a kindness. But excessive use of cosmetics can be offensive to grieving relatives. I recall viewing my grandmother's body following her death to discover that this elderly lady, who rarely used make-up in her lifetime, had been smothered in lipstick and rouge, and

watched my distressed mother painstakingly wipe it off her dead mother's face with a tissue.

Gathering round a body in a chapel of rest will invariably provoke an outpouring of grief. Grief may be punctuated by comments of how peaceful the dead person looks. In death the facial muscles relax, wrinkles and frowns disappear and a person can look not only peaceful but years younger. If death occurred after a long and painful illness, the sight of the person in repose is likely to be a source of consolation to a grieving relative. When a death is sudden or unexpected it can sometimes help a bereaved friend or relative to write a letter to the deceased and place it in the coffin. Standing around the body, memories surface and there is likely to be laughter as well as tears. But sometimes there can be anger too. It is not unknown for the sight of the corpse to unleash a torrent of frustration and pent-up rage in a relative. Words and thoughts not uttered during the person's lifetime now spill out in fury. In death it is safe to say things that in life were bottled up.

If this happens it is vital not to stop or stifle it, or feel embarrassed or shocked by it. There is catharsis in these outpourings. By definition, grief is anarchic and appears in various guises, including fear, frustration, anguish, resentment and bafflement. Eventually the anger will subside or just peter out, perhaps with the relative just quietly sobbing, their anger spent. In such a situation the role of the minister is to witness and to hold the bereaved in prayer before God as they begin to come to terms with the death and what it represents for them. It will also be for the minister to judge if and when to offer to say a prayer, whether to withdraw and leave the distressed relative alone or whether gently to lead the person out.

The psalms are a wonderful resource in these situations. They are rich with the language of lament and full of questions: How long, O Lord? Why? They address God head-on and do not shrink from expressing desolation in the face of death and loss. They rage against the absence of God: 'My tears have been my bread day and night, while all day long they say to me, "Where is now your God?" (Ps. 42.3). The psalms invite us to present our chaos before God and beseech his mercy in the faith that just as

the Spirit moved over the waters of chaos in the act of creation, bringing forth light and order and peace, so God will bring order and healing to our lives and memories. A list of suitable psalms is included in Appendix C.

Healing memories

In any meeting with the bereaved, particularly in a first encounter when feelings may be raw, it is important to exercise self-discipline both in what we say and in our body language so that we do not inadvertently signal that what is being shared is inappropriate and ought not to be expressed or is simply boring. We need to take care about the questions we ask and the comments we make. Questions need to be open-ended and never intrusive. Planning a funeral is often left to the women in the family. Men may not be used to articulating their feelings, certainly not in front of a stranger. If they are made to feel uncomfortable they are likely to shut down instantly. Similarly, if we make the bereaved feel ashamed or guilty about expressing grief or anger (or indeed their relief that someone has died), it will postpone their coming to terms with what has happened.

There is often anxiety about expressing sadness today, as if admitting to it constitutes a negative statement about oneself. Many feel ashamed, embarrassed, inadequate and in some indefinable way, a failure. Sadness has become a taboo subject. We even use the term pejoratively: 'He's a sad case' or 'That's a sad thing to say'. It is as if there is a prohibition gathering around the word itself. Feeling sad or being angry does not demean us, but the bereaved may need permission to feel and admit these things and in so doing be helped to hold more than one emotion at any given time. They may also need permission to cry, particularly the men. 'Don't try to be too brave', is good advice as a family prepares for a funeral.

We all tell our stories with their instinctive emphases, distortions and omissions. Sometimes we use them to maintain grievance, to justify ourselves or to put another person in the wrong, including the deceased. We can harbour resentment without consciously

knowing it. All of us lodge painful memories and in bereavement these are likely to bubble to the surface. As half-buried memories are disinterred they often stir up feelings of remorse. But remorse can unlock a new future by enabling us to come to terms with the past and attend to things we feel guilty about. In other words, although bereavement is painful, by the grace of God it can also open us to profound inner healing.

The prayers during the funeral service in *Common Worship* are structured around a series of petitions, the last of which includes a prayer for the healing of memories. To be meaningful, each of the set petitions needs to be personalized by the officiating minister, and either introduced informally or at least embroidered. The final petition in particular is best prefaced with a sensitive but specific invitation to the congregation to lay their memories of the deceased before God: things that were never said but should have been, and things that were said in haste or in anger and are now regretted. Things can't be unsaid in life. Words can hurt and damage. The minister then needs to pause to allow space for recollection before closing with these or other appropriate words:

> [Lord,] You are tender towards your children
> and your mercy is over all your works.
> Heal any memories of hurt and failure.
> Give us the wisdom and grace to use aright
> the time that is left to us here on earth,
> to turn to Christ and follow in his steps
> in the way that leads to everlasting life. (p. 281)

The same prayer can be used in the run-up to the funeral. In all meetings and conversations with the bereaved, and supremely in the context of the funeral liturgy, a minister needs to foster a culture of honest recollection in which painful memories can be disinterred and left at the foot of the cross where they belong. The goal of such prayerful reflection is not the erasing of memories, which is neither possible nor desirable, but their healing. At the heart of the Christian message and of all funeral ministry is the good news of the forgiveness of God.

5

Death, children and funerals

No more shall there be in [the city]
an infant that lives but a few days,
or an old person who does not live out a lifetime;
for one who dies at a hundred years will be
  considered a youth,
and one who falls short of a hundred will be
  considered accursed.
They shall build houses and inhabit them;
they shall plant vineyards and eat their fruit.
They shall not build and another inhabit;
they shall not plant and another eat;
for like the days of a tree shall the days of my people be,
and my chosen shall long enjoy the work of their hands.
They shall not labour in vain,
or bear children for calamity;
for they shall be offspring blessed by the LORD –
and their descendants as well.

Isaiah 65.20–23

The death of a child is always a tragedy. In the scheme of things, children bury their parents, not the other way round. Rates of infant mortality may be low in this country but that does not diminish the impact of the loss of a child on parents and siblings. In fact parents may never come to terms with their loss, or at least not entirely. One Boxing Day I remember my own mother aged 75 weeping about her first child who died in infancy, remarking that had my elder brother Peter lived he would have been 50 that day. Inevitably, when parents lose a baby or a child they ask a

host of questions. Some will be practical questions, perhaps relating to the care – or perceived lack of it – that their child received. Did the hospital do everything in its power to save him/her? Was the doctor or midwife negligent in any way? In an age marked by huge medical advancements, the fact that certain illnesses cannot be cured and that children die can come as a profound shock. There is also likely to be a raft of personal questions. Why us and our baby/child? What did we do wrong? Are we being punished? The perennial question about why a loving God should permit suffering in the world is sharpened when it is asked in relation to the death of a child. With the prophet Isaiah we look forward to the time when children are not born 'for calamity' and no longer 'shall there be . . . an infant that lives but a few days'. It is not just we who weep with those who weep: God does too.

The funeral of a child

Inevitably the way we minister to parents and siblings mourning the death of their teenage daughter in a car accident will be different from the way we minister to a family whose five-year-old child has died in hospital from cancer after enduring long and painful treatments, or to a young couple mourning the loss of their premature baby. The funerals of these children are likely to be radically different. In the case of the first there is likely to be a church full of distressed classmates. In the case of the death of a premature baby it is likely that only the parents will be present in the crematorium chapel, with perhaps either the father or mother carrying the little coffin containing their child's body. For them, the unknown is likely to be one of the hardest things to bear: the sense of not knowing what the child's life would have been like had she or he lived. With them, we grieve the loss of potential. Just because a life has been cut short does not mean it is worthless.

In the case of the stillborn it is not unusual for grief to be suppressed. Ministers can find themselves conducting private services for a grieving parent months later. When a child has been

aborted, grief and guilt can mingle and go underground because the event cannot easily be admitted. It may be years before grief finally breaks through the carapace of shame into the light of day, seeking healing. One minister described conducting a private service for a woman years after a stillbirth and how afterwards, standing in the churchyard, they released a helium balloon with the name of the child written on a label attached to it. The woman commented how helpful it was to have something visible to hold and to kiss in place of the baby she had never cuddled, and then to let it go.

With the funeral of a child, *Common Worship* retains the same liturgical structure as that designed for an adult, while recognizing that the words the minister uses to introduce the service, including verses from Scripture, need to be chosen sensitively, according to the age of the child and the circumstances of his or her death. Words from St John's First Letter may be particularly appropriate: 'Beloved, we are God's children now; what we will be has not yet been revealed. What we do know is this: when he is revealed, we will be like him, for we will see him as he is' (1 John 3.2). It offers a range of resources for such a funeral,[1] including a variety of prayers that may be said by grieving parents, including this:

> God of love and life,
> you gave N to us as our *son/daughter*.
> Give us now the assurance
> that though *he/she* has passed from our sight,
> *he/she* has not passed from your care.
> Draw near to us in our sadness,
> bring blessing out of grief,
> and help us in our tears and pain
> to know you standing alongside us
> and to experience your love and healing;
> through Jesus Christ our Lord. **Amen.** (p. 306)

---

1 *Common Worship: Pastoral Services* (2000), London: CHP, pp. 301–15.

As with any funeral, the resources *Common Worship* offers will always need to be adapted and supplemented according to circumstances. There are numerous published liturgical resources and an extensive literature about patterns of bereavement following the death of a child, including the often unacknowledged impact of such a death on siblings. Attention tends to focus on the parents, but brothers and sisters can equally be affected. Furthermore grieving parents can unwittingly project on to their remaining child or children expectations and hopes that belonged to their dead child. These then feel pressurized to perform/succeed on behalf of their dead sibling. Clergy who are privileged to have a church school at which a grieving sibling may be a pupil will have a unique opportunity to work in partnership with teachers in the support of the child in the months following a funeral.

Children attending funerals

There is no norm when it comes to children attending and/or participating in funerals. In some cultures women and children never attend a funeral. A funeral is the province of men. This is not normally the case in Britain except in some Scottish communities, but there will always be a debate about the appropriateness of children attending a funeral. Some parents may opt to bring their children to the church for the service but hesitate to take them to a crematorium or cemetery. Others will include the children in everything lest excluding them only succeeds in generating fear of the unknown. Much, of course, will depend on a child's age and temperament. Some parents will instinctively be protective of their family. Others will take a more matter-of-fact view and feel that children should not be wrapped in cotton wool, and will let them decide for themselves.

Children are certainly more robust and resilient than we often give them credit for. I recall the funeral of a young man at which his eight-year-old son movingly placed a rose on his father's coffin during the service. As the boy had watched his father grow steadily weaker from cancer over an 18-month

period, his exclusion from the funeral would have been a terrible mistake. Like everyone else there, he too needed to let go and say goodbye to his dad.

Every parent wants their child to be happy, but part of growing up includes coming to terms with the unpalatable fact that sad and bad things happen, and sometimes they happen to really good people like one's mum or dad. On the list of things we all have to come to terms with is death. A child is more likely to encounter it through the death of a pet than a parent, and the event should not be glossed over. The death of a pet hamster or discovering a dead pigeon in the park are golden opportunities for parents to enter into conversation with their children about what happens when something or someone dies. My parents recall the death of Sparky our budgerigar when I was a little boy. I remember we put him in an empty Milk Tray chocolates box and buried him under the cherry tree in the back garden and said the Lord's Prayer together. It was my first funeral.

Coping with loss in all its manifestations is part of growing up. Enabling children to handle this without frightening them, answering their questions as best one can, equipping them with a vocabulary with which they can reflect on their experience and praying with them all helps to lay down solid foundations for later life and will enable them to handle bereavement better as adults. Too often the 'spirituality' adults offer children equates to lighting candles and giving daffodils on Mothering Sunday, but fails to relate to loss, suffering and death. We do them a disservice when we serve up a spiritual diet of marzipan.

Psychologists tell us that by and large children do not necessarily relate to anxiety but they do understand fear. In general, when a death occurs it is therefore far the best course to tell children what has happened simply and straightforwardly, without recourse to euphemisms, and to explain as best one can what is going to happen next. Children are naturally intuitive as well as inquisitive, and will immediately detect half-truths and dissembling. Being overprotective or assuming that a child is too young to understand is likely to backfire.

The questions children ask

One of the most challenging experiences I had as a young priest was being present at the death of a father from renal failure. The doctors fought long and hard to keep him alive in the hope that a suitable donor might be found to permit a kidney transplant. In the event none was found. His condition deteriorated, he slipped into unconsciousness and late one Ash Wednesday evening he died. His wife, who had kept vigil beside his hospital bed for days, was distraught. Meanwhile their little boy sat in the waiting room with his grandparents, unaware of the gravity of his father's condition. His mother asked me to break the news to her son, saying that she was too upset to do so herself. Squatting down on the floor next to the lad, I began a conversation about the truck with which he was playing, and taking advantage of a lull in the conversation and an enquiring look in his eyes, I shared the news of his dad's death. It was one of the most painful things I have ever had to do.

I think too of my first week as a vicar in north London and the death of a local teenager from a massive brain haemorrhage. He had been a hero of the football field, and the headteacher of the church school his younger twin brothers attended asked me to break the news of Eddie's death to the assembled children and to field any questions. Their questions were terrifying in their direct-ness. Children don't function in grey areas but relate solely to the concrete. Our responses need to be framed with that in mind. Situations like this can arise at any time in any context, be it over a family meal, in school or at church. Of course, we will never get it right. We can only do our best and speak words that are true for us, and if we don't know the answer, say so.

Here are some of the questions that may pop up, together with some possible, if inadequate, responses:

Why do we die?

As we grow older our bodies grow tired and sometimes we become ill. When this happens we go to see the doctor or, if it is serious, we go into hospital. The doctors and nurses who

work in hospitals work hard to make sick and injured people better. Usually they can help heal us, but sometimes our bodies are so old or worn out that they can't mend them any more and we die.

What happens to us when we die?

Our bodies stop working. Our heart stops beating and pumping the blood round our bodies and we stop breathing.

Why can't doctors stop us from dying?

Doctors and nurses work hard to help us live long and healthy lives. They have all sorts of medicines to help us get better when we are ill. Sometimes though, even when they have done their very best, they can't help a person and that person dies.

Does it hurt when you die?

Doctors tell us that death isn't usually painful. Even when someone dies in a car crash or in an accident, everything happens so fast that they feel virtually nothing at all. If a person is ill in hospital or has to have an operation, the doctors and nurses have special medicines that can take away most of the pain. So there is nothing to fear. When we die it is a bit like going to sleep, except when we wake up we find ourselves in the arms of God.

Why does God let people die?

God loves us always throughout our life, from the moment we are born. When our bodies wear out and we die, God doesn't stop loving us.

Why do some people die when they are young?

We don't always know. Sometimes it's because their bodies weren't properly made when they were babies. Sometimes it's because they

have caught a disease for which the doctors have not yet found a cure, which makes their bodies stop working properly.

What happens to someone's body when they die?

They don't need their body any more, so we are having a special wooden box made to put it in called a coffin. Then we are going to have a special service to thank God for that person's life and to ask God to look after them. We will then say goodbye and bury the coffin in the ground. (or: We are then going to say goodbye and take their body to a special place called a crematorium, where it will be turned into ashes, and then we will bury the ashes in the ground.) Just as a caterpillar goes to sleep in a chrysalis and is transformed into a beautiful butterfly, so we believe that one day God will make a new beautiful body for N, just as he did for Jesus.

Where is he/she now?

He/she is in the arms of God and God is looking after him/her for us. We call that place heaven. We have passed him/her into God's care, who wants the very best for all of us; that is why we are called to trust him.

Will I ever see N again (the person who has died)?

When we die we don't come back to this life again. It's why people get upset and cry. We are sad when someone we love dies and we miss them a lot. But we also believe that because they are with God, and God is always with us, they too are with us in a special way. We can't always see our friends but we know that they love us and care for us. Although we can no longer see N, we believe he/she is a friend of Jesus and still loves us just as much as we still love him/her.

Is my pet in heaven?

God loves all his creatures. He loves you and me and N. God looks after all of us, including N.

Are you going to die (often addressed to parents)?

None of us knows how long we are going to live, but probably it will be for a very long time. It's why I pray to God every day for his help so that whatever happens I trust him and am not afraid.

Am I going to die?

One day, but not yet. We are all going to die one day, but that's a long, long way away; so there is nothing to be frightened of.

6

The context we set

For everything there is a season,
and a time for every matter under heaven:
a time to be born, and a time to die.

Ecclesiastes 3.1

The majority of the population today instinctively turn to the internet for information, including what to do in the face of death. Parishes that have up-to-date websites are immediately at an advantage, which is why it would be good if all church websites carried basic information about what options are available to people when planning a funeral, who to contact and what Christians believe about death and life after death. We need to be better at communicating with the general public and marketing ourselves, otherwise we will always be vulnerable to what others claim we believe and to the destructive power of misinformation.

What our buildings can offer

Why are we such shy advocates of what our buildings can offer? Unlike crematoria, where the slot allowed for a funeral is strictly limited and seating is restricted, our churches offer huge flexibility. We have far more space available and can allow the service much more time. When a funeral takes place entirely at the crematorium, a family can ask for a longer slot than is customary and this can be arranged by negotiation, but it is likely to incur additional charges. We need to be upbeat and more positive about our buildings and encourage people to come into church for their funeral. If we don't do this, whole rafts of people will never have

had cause to cross the threshold of our buildings, which will further erode the culture of churchgoing. Church will be something other people do, a private club in which 'we' have no place. A bereaved family is more likely to bring the children back for a Harvest Festival or a Christingle service later in the year if they have had a positive experience of being inside the church for their aunt's funeral. Church will feel less alien, less threatening.

Taking funeral ministry seriously should give added impetus to making our buildings fit for purpose in the twenty-first century. Clergy like to caricature crematoria as clinical and factory-like, but many young people respond positively to their modern décor. They are clean, comfortable and contemporary. By contrast, too many of our church buildings are dirty, uncomfortable and old-fashioned. They are poorly lit and ill-equipped, with no toilet and with facilities that are badly in need of updating. The home team do not always see this, confusing the smell of damp hassocks with the odour of sanctity. Strangers see our buildings with clearer eyes.

Getting the welcome right

The context we set for a funeral in church begins at the church door with the welcome we extend to the bereaved. Every congregation likes to think of itself as warm, welcoming and friendly, but this is not necessarily the experience of visitors. Regular churchgoers soon forget how scary it can be for someone unfamiliar with the rituals and customs of Anglican worship to cross the threshold of a church. Vast numbers of the population have had little or no contact with the church for generations. Attending a funeral in a church can be an intimidating experience as well as an emotional one.

Well before the service is scheduled to start it is important that adequate parking be reserved for the hearse and cars carrying the immediate family. In inner-city parishes where there are parking restrictions, this may entail the funeral director or someone from the church contacting the local council beforehand to suspend

sufficient parking bays. If need be, delegate a member of the congregation to patrol the road and ward off overzealous traffic wardens. It doesn't help if grieving relatives emerge at the end of the service en route to the crematorium to find their cars festooned with parking tickets.

It is also important to reserve sufficient seating at the front of the church for the family and immediate mourners, and to make sure they are equipped with orders of service. As far as possible it is good to gauge accurate numbers to avoid overestimating the seating required and leaving empty pews behind the immediate family, who then feel exposed. The sensitive meeting and greeting of people as they arrive, offering warmth without being effusive, will set the tone for what follows, as will the quality of personal preparation a minister brings to the funeral. The way we look and lead the service, speak, preach, move and hold ourselves will all enhance or detract from it. So will the way the organ is played, supporting the singing without dominating it. How visitors are treated, many of whom may never have been in a church before, will affect how they remember the occasion. In fact sometimes this can count as much as the actual service. All these things contribute to the experience of church and will affect the credibility of our mission.

Modern technology

Many crematoria now offer screens or digital projectors for use in funeral services. Civil celebrants often use these to show digital pictorial biographies of the deceased, set to music. A church equipped with modern technology and overhead projection can permit a similarly imaginative approach to funeral ministry, displaying photographs of the deceased and their family during or before the service. Families sometimes create these biographies themselves, but there are individuals and firms willing to take on this work on their behalf. Requests for the incorporation of such digital media at funerals are likely to grow increasingly common in future years. It will not be appropriate in every context, but sometimes it can be very moving.

At the funeral of my uncle, before the service started and as people gathered, a sequence of photographs from his life were projected in a loop on a drop-down screen at the front of the nave while the organ played. There were photographs from his childhood and upbringing, his service in the RAF, his subsequent career, marriage and family life. Far from being intrusive or tacky, it set the tone for what followed and created an atmosphere of warmth and recollection. Orders of service bearing a photograph of the deceased on the front cover or an enlarged photograph on a noticeboard visible on entering the church can similarly help personalize a funeral.

Preparing an order of service

The bespoke nature of funerals today means that parishes need to rise to the challenge of producing attractive orders of service. Ideally these should contain all the hymns and readings and be something mourners can take away with them and treasure as a remembrance of the occasion. This is what many civil celebrants do, and the Church needs to do it better. Some funeral directors offer to print an order of service for their clients, but it is much better if a church takes responsibility for its own funerals so that the literature produced and distributed is not only seemly but consciously furthers mission. Small or rural churches may find this over-the-top and time-consuming, but it need not be as onerous as it sounds.

Ideally a church needs to identify someone in the congregation who is computer-literate and who with guidance can develop a basic template for its funeral services. Into this template can then be slotted hymns and readings as required. Parishes that do not have photocopying facilities can either appeal to a neighbouring parish for help or take their bespoke order of service to a local printer. Alternatively a group of parishes or even a deanery could be encouraged to collaborate in such a venture and produce orders of service that are inexpensive but of good quality.

It is a good idea for an order of service to carry information about church services, perhaps on the back cover, together with contact details of the church and clergy. *Common Worship* provides a 'Pastoral introduction' to a funeral service, which deserves to be used more widely. Its text is printed at the end of this chapter. Some churches print it – together with words of welcome from the incumbent of the parish – on the inside cover of an order of service for people to read as they wait for the funeral to begin. Alternatively a parish could include a brief statement of Christian belief of its own choosing. All these things add value to the 'church experience' and sow seeds that, God willing, will germinate later in a desire to explore the Christian faith.

Retiring collections

In planning a service it is important to raise with the bereaved family their wishes about a retiring collection. It is entirely appropriate for a parish to put out a plate at the back of the church, complete with Gift Aid envelopes, and to invite donations towards the mission and ministry of the church. A family may even be happy that a note to this effect should be printed in the order of service. Equally a family may wish there to be a retiring collection in aid, say, of the local hospice where the person died or a named charity the deceased supported. They may already have talked about this with the funeral director.

In such circumstances it is good practice to have two plates, one for the church and one for the designated charity, each clearly labelled, so that there is no confusion in the minds of donors about which fund they are contributing to. This also saves any embarrassment at the back of the church afterwards while the verger and the funeral director squabble over the collection and who is taking care of it. The funeral director can take responsibility on behalf of the family for any donations to the charity, and the church can take responsibility for its own monies in the normal way.

It is important for a church to have a policy about retiring collections, including how monies are to be recorded and distributed after the service. Doing things on an ad hoc basis at the back of the church just raises people's blood pressure. It is good practice for there to be a PCC resolution on such collections – legally the purpose of any collection, other than at services of Holy Communion, needs to be determined by the PCC and incumbent jointly. It makes sense for such a resolution to be couched in general rather than specific terms, otherwise any charity or good cause not listed would require a further resolution of the PCC. Hence a PCC might agree that additional names could be annexed to the authorized list by the authority of the churchwardens and incumbent. The advantage of such a procedure is that it creates an administrative and legal buffer between a bereaved family and the incumbent, so that if a family proposes – or the deceased proposed – a charity with which the parish priest is unhappy, he or she can take refuge in the PCC resolution, as well as ecclesiastical law, for protection and so defuse any argument.

Pastoral Introduction[1]

This may be read by those present before the funeral begins.

God's love and power extend over all creation. Every life, including our own, is precious to God. Christians have always believed that there is hope in death as in life, and that there is new life in Christ after death.

Even those who share such faith find that there is a real sense of loss at the death of a loved one. We will each have had our own experiences of their life and death, with different memories and different feelings of love, grief and respect. To acknowledge this at the beginning of the service should help us to use this occasion to express our faith and our feelings as we say farewell, to acknowledge our loss and our sorrow, and to reflect on our own mortality. Those who mourn need support and consolation. Our presence here today is part of that continuing support.

---

[1] *Common Worship: Pastoral Services* (2000), London: CHP, p. 256.

7

The funeral service

God be in my head,
and in my understanding.
God be in my eyes,
and in my looking.
God be in my mouth,
and in my speaking.
God be in my heart,
and in my loving.
God be at mine end,
and at my departing.

from the *Sarum Primer* (1514)

An Anglican funeral (whether held in a church or at a crematorium), no less than a 'secular' funeral conducted by a humanist or civil celebrant, can and should be tailored to the requirements of the bereaved. The funeral of Diana, Princess of Wales, in Westminster Abbey was described at the time as 'unique as befits the unique person she was'. But every person is unique in God's eyes. If the Church of England can do it for royalty and the famous, then we can and should do it for the old gentleman who lived locally and ran the corner shop. We need to nail our reputation for stuffiness and inflexibility.

In many ways Princess Diana's funeral in 1997 represented a watershed in public awareness of the way a funeral service can be shaped. The service included a personal tribute from Earl Spencer, Diana's brother. Elton John reworked his song, 'Candle in the Wind'. Originally it had been written to celebrate the life of Marilyn Monroe; now it was sung in honour of Diana and renamed, 'Goodbye England's Rose'. As her coffin was led out

of the Abbey, the choir sang John Taverner's 'Song for Athene', blending Scripture, liturgical texts and Orthodox alleluias in salutation. The service was highly charged and highly eclectic, but it caught the national mood at the time and 'ticked the box'. Overnight, as it were, it gave permission for people to do something similarly imaginative for their loved ones.

In Canon Law only an ordained minister may officiate at a burial of a body in consecrated ground, and thus by extension at a funeral. In most dioceses, however, the bishop may authorize a Reader or lay worker, after appropriate training, also to bury the dead and officiate at cremations, though they may only do so at the invitation of the minister of the parish and with the goodwill of the family concerned. In some deaneries the participation of Readers and lay ministers in the church's funeral ministry, far from being incidental, has become valued and indispensable, not least with the reduction in the number of stipendiary clergy. Bespoke funeral services require huge preparation, and hard-pressed clergy cannot easily sustain a large number of funerals without the overall pattern of their ministry becoming distorted. The days of the 'bog-standard Church of England funeral' have gone.

Continuity and change in funeral rites

This book is not a liturgical or historical study, but even a cursory survey of the development of English funeral rites reveals the extent to which funerals have changed over the centuries and are continuing to evolve. Some changes have been driven by a shift in doctrine, as at the Reformation; others have been prompted by national mood, as with Princess Diana's death or the massive loss of life during the First World War; yet others have come in response to changing fashions, such as the revival of cremation. Funeral rites have always adjusted to new circumstances, and it may be that we are witnessing another huge cultural shift that needs to be met with a fresh application of liturgical imagination and pastoral sensitivity.

The medieval rite was as much, if not more, for the person who had died as for those mourning the passing of their relative or friend. The prayers of the Church both militant here on earth and triumphant in heaven were to assist them on their journey to God. When Cranmer translated the burial service into English in 1549, he simplified the ceremonial. He expunged any reference to purgatory, though retained – at least at first – cautious petitions for the departed. The atmosphere of the new rite was characterized by a restored emphasis on rest in Christ and resurrection to life. In the medieval rite the words spoken in Latin by the priest upon greeting the coffin were taken from Psalm 116: 'The snares of death encompassed me; the pains of hell took hold of me; by grief and sorrow was I held.' In the new rite the priest spoke words from St John's Gospel that remain a hallmark of Anglican funeral liturgy:

The priest metyng the corps at the churche style, shalt say; Or els the priestes and clerkes shalt sing, and so goe either into the churche or towardes the grave:

> I am the resurreccion and the life (sayth the Lord): he that beleveth in me, yea though he were dead, yet shall he live. And whosoever lyveth and beleveth in me shall not dye for ever.

In later Anglican prayer books, under pressure from evangelical Christians, further liturgical changes were made and the burial service was truncated. Public petitions for the departed were now removed both from funerals and from the conclusion of the 'Prayer for the Church Militant' in the order for Holy Communion. These modest excisions did not go far enough for some Reformers.[1] The funeral is not for the dead, they argued, but for the living, and for that reason should be avoided altogether. Thus the Puritan Westminster Directory of Public Worship, approved by an ordinance

---

1 For a survey of medieval, Reformation and Post-Reformation funeral rites, see Geoffrey Rowell (1977), *The Liturgy of Christian Burial*, London: Alcuin Club/SPCK, pp. 57–98.

of Parliament in 1645 to replace the Book of Common Prayer, forbade all burial services. The Directory decreed that the bodies of the dead were to be interred without ceremony, prayer, the reading of Scripture or even preaching. Paradoxically, particularly given the current public debate about the place of religion in national life, the Puritans argued that burial was a purely secular matter. From a pastoral perspective informed by the insights of psychology into the grieving process, such an attitude to funerals is open to severe criticism. Today the vast majority of Christians are united in valuing a funeral service, even if they may have different views about whether the service is primarily for the benefit of the living, the dead or both.

Some of the Puritan objections to the Prayer Book burial office resurfaced at the Savoy Conference in 1661 following the restoration of the monarchy. One of their criticisms was the 'skudding' of the minister to the church lychgate to meet the funeral cortège and lead the coffin in procession into church or to the grave. Seen against this acrimonious backcloth, the burial service as eventually authorized in the Book of Common Prayer of 1662 seems theologically rich and generous in its provision. By modern standards, however, for all the elegance of the language, its austerity no longer meets the pastoral needs of the general population, which is neither confident in its Christian identity nor articulate about the faith it professes. In the Prayer Book service there is no commendation of the departed. There is no provision even for the name of the deceased to be mentioned, though it is impossible to know if this was ever adhered to in practice. Instead the minister is restricted to talking about 'our dear brother/sister here departed'. In fact it was not until the liturgical revisions of 1965 that the possibility of actually mentioning the deceased by name was sanctioned again. When families and funeral directors criticize the impersonal character of some Anglican funerals today, what they may be smarting at is a regimented use by some clergy of the Prayer Book burial service without recourse to any of the liturgical modifications and flexibility as proposed in either the 1928 or 1965 revisions. These liturgical revisions provided alternative psalms, readings and prayers for the bereaved, together with occasional material. Petitions for the

departed had been reinstated in 1928, partly through the convictions of Anglo-Catholics but in reality as a way of coping with the weight of grief following the carnage of the First World War. When people today request a traditional 'Prayer Book funeral', it is likely that they are referring to the 1928 rite (subsequently also known as the First Series), not to the more austere 1662 burial service.

The funeral in *Common Worship*

What is the purpose of a funeral? *Common Worship: Pastoral Services*, which includes the new funeral service as well as other valuable liturgical resources for use with the dying and at memorial services, has been authorized for use in the Church of England since 2000. It sets out an answer to this question in the introduction, which the minister is required to give or to adapt at the beginning of the service:

> We have come here today
> to remember before God our *brother/sister* N;
> to give thanks for *his/her* life;
> to commend *him/her* to God our merciful redeemer and judge;
> to commit *his/her* body to be *buried/cremated*,
> and to comfort one another in our grief. (p. 276)

To meet the needs of our generation, *Common Worship* provides an authorized structure for a funeral service, but with huge flexibility in how it should be organized. This allows a minister freedom to construct a service suited to the occasion, but he or she should never lose sight of the declared purposes of a funeral as set out in this introduction.

Common Worship recognizes that not only is burial no longer the norm in Britain today, but that the sequence of events that go to make a funeral may not be seamless or liturgically tidy. Geography will be as much a factor in fashioning the practicalities of a funeral as theological sensibilities. Certain parts of the Anglican funeral service, such as the Commendation and Fare-

well, and the Committal, have authorized words. These are the strong moments in the service that require dignity and formality. But elsewhere *Common Worship* provides a wide selection of prayers and psalms, together with suggestions for readings from Scripture that a minister can and should adapt and supplement according to pastoral need. The recommended structure is as follows:

- **The Gathering**
  There must be a welcome from the officiating minister, followed by an introduction to the service. Prayers of Penitence may be used. The Gathering concludes with the Collect, which may be one of the set prayers or else one taken from the compendium of collects and prayers at the back of *Common Worship*. This leads naturally into a hymn.
- **Readings and Sermon**
  There must be at least one reading from Scripture, and in most funerals this is preceded by a psalm (usually the twenty-third psalm), which may be said or sung. If there are two readings, the psalm can be recited between the two. Provision is made for a eulogy but this is not a substitute for a sermon.
- **Prayers**
  A format for intercession is provided, which needs to be tailored to the occasion and, above all, made personal.
- **Commendation and Farewell**
  Whether this occurs in a church or crematorium chapel, it is a key moment in the service that should not be hurried. Authorized words must be used.
- **The Committal**
  This will vary according to whether the body is to be buried or cremated, and whether the service takes place in church or entirely at the crematorium. Again, authorized words must be used.
- **The Dismissal**
  Bringing the service to a fitting close is important. The dismissal is not just symbolic: it is about enabling a family to 'let go' and to 'move on'.

In this country, black remains the most commonly worn colour at funerals by mourners. However, in reaction to the Victorian way of death with its elaborate funeral processions complete with dyed ostrich feathers, mutes and yards of black crepe, it is no longer unusual for a family to request that no black should be worn, or even to stipulate bright colours. This is particularly the case with the funerals of children and young people. This can be a helpful counterbalance to a pattern of mourning that could be stultifying and border on the hypocritical. However, the pendulum may be swinging too far. We need to be alert equally to the danger of excluding or trivializing grief.

If a family has been alongside the person during a long and painful terminal illness it is likely that much of their grieving will already have occurred by the time death comes. Instinctively they tend to plan the funeral as a celebration of the person's life. Although this is understandable, the family may need help in realizing that the rest of the community may not be at the same stage and may still be in shock or grief. In such circumstances, overcelebratory funerals may need scaling back to accommodate the diverse needs of those present. As the poet Roger McGough says in the opening stanza of his poem 'I am not Sleeping',[2] parodying 'life-centred' funerals, a life is not to be celebrated but rather mourned 'till it hurts'. Fudging the reality of death only cheapens the life we commemorate. Expectations vary enormously, from those wanting a funeral in church to those who prefer the service to be held entirely at the crematorium or cemetery chapel, or more rarely just at the graveside. The bereaved may request that a funeral take place in the context of a celebration of the Eucharist, which may be termed a Requiem. If the deceased was a regular communicant this can be particularly appropriate. For the last time it brings them back into the heart of the church where they worshipped, surrounded by their brothers and sisters in Christ. Meanwhile families of African or Caribbean descent may request

---

2 Roger McGough (2006), from 'I Am Not Sleeping', *Selected Poems*, London: Penguin.

an open coffin, with the whole congregation filing past during the Commendation and Farewell to pay their final respects.

There will always be circumstances where it is necessary for a burial or cremation to take place in advance of a funeral service, for example when a person dies abroad and the body cannot easily be repatriated. However, it is becoming increasingly common for some families, including those who are committed and practising Christians, to request that the Committal – usually a cremation – take place privately in advance of the funeral. The funeral is then held later in the day and takes on the character of a thanksgiving service for the person's life. At this service there is no coffin because the body has already been buried or cremated. As a result emotions tend to get compartmentalized, with sad feelings being deposited at the crematorium along with the body. At the service that follows, people are then encouraged by the family to be altogether more positive and upbeat.

However desirable it is to meet with generosity the requests of the bereaved, this particular request should be treated cautiously if not resisted. It is usually designed to minimize upset and accommodate the needs of hospitality for mourners who have travelled long distances, particularly where the crematorium is miles from either the church or the wake. A family may be anxious that by the time they return from the crematorium the congregation will have dispersed. These are legitimate concerns that need to be addressed and ways round them found, but not at the expense of compartmentalizing the funeral. For example, some members of the family could be deputed to stay behind after the funeral to greet people and not go on to the crematorium for the Committal. Alternatively, it is perfectly possible to have an interval between the funeral service and the Committal in order to permit the family to greet people, and then for just the immediate family to go to the crematorium.

The real objection to a private Committal in advance of a funeral service is that it disables the majority of mourners from coming to terms with the death. It is their loss too, not just that of the immediate family, and they need to say their own goodbyes.

Seeing the coffin brings home the reality of death. Its absence can confuse people and inhibit their grieving. When we attempt to compartmentalize feelings in this way or tidy death away, we end up damaging ourselves. Jeremy Brooks, in his study of funeral ministry, also points out how unsatisfactory from a theological perspective is the absence of the coffin at a funeral, pointing out that at the heart of the Christian faith is a belief in the resurrection of the body, not the migration of souls. He argues:

> Our bodies matter in our faith, and by excluding them from their own funerals, we undermine their importance. The Christian pilgrimage or journey begins at our baptism – whether that is as a baby in a font or as a believer in a baptistery pool – and ends at our funeral. Surely we should mark that ending as we marked the beginning, by being present in our coffins before the altar of God?[3]

Receiving the coffin in church

Either the will left by the deceased, or the bereaved family, may request that the coffin be brought into church in advance of the funeral. This could be earlier in the day of the funeral or the evening before, perhaps at the conclusion of Evening Prayer. It is particularly appropriate when the deceased was a loyal member of the church or where a family would value the opportunity for quiet reflection in advance of what might be a 'big' funeral the next day. A church is a gentler space for recollection and saying personal goodbyes than the funeral director's chapel of rest. It can help with the shock of seeing the coffin *in situ*. It also opens the possibility for a vigil of prayer in circumstances where the death was a traumatic event in the life of a family or local community, relieving some of the pressure that otherwise would be funnelled into

---

3 Jeremy Brooks (2013), *Heaven's Morning Breaks*, Stowmarket: Kevin Mayhew, p. 22.

the service itself. Receiving the body in church in advance of the funeral can also be helpful to young children attending a funeral for the first time. They can be brought into church in advance of the service to familiarize themselves with the building, their questions can be answered and – it is hoped – any concerns allayed.

Common Worship provides a brief order of service for the reception of a body in advance of the funeral, which can be adapted if the ceremony follows or is joined to Evening Prayer or Compline. As at a funeral, the immediate family may wish to follow the coffin into church or be seated in advance. If customary, at the entry to the church the priest may sprinkle the coffin with water from the font in remembrance of the person's baptism. The priest then leads the coffin to the top of the nave, reciting sentences of Scripture in the usual way. The coffin is normally placed longwise at the front of the nave, feet facing east. By custom, the coffins of clergy are placed the other way round, their feet facing their congregation. Funeral directors normally come with trestles in two sizes: tall and short. If the custom is to cover the coffin with a pall (see below), tall trestles will be necessary. Otherwise shorter trestles may be more convenient.

Some parishes and funeral directors retain a pall to cover the coffin, though this has become unfashionable in an age that values simplicity. The word 'pall' derives from the Latin *pallium*, meaning 'cloak', and refers to any cloth that envelops or covers an object. In the context of a funeral, the word refers to the large, heavy hanging that is used to cover the coffin. It may be of black, purple or dark red material, or occasionally white, and may be embroidered with a cross or other Christian symbols. Military funerals invariably cover the coffin with the Union flag. Members of the family, friends or members of the congregation may wish to join in placing the pall over the coffin. Words in *Common Worship*, adapted from Isaiah 25.7–8, may be spoken: 'On Mount Zion the Lord will remove the pall of sorrow hanging over all nations. He will destroy death for ever: he will wipe away the tears from every face.' In addition to a pall and flowers, a Bible or cross may be placed on or near the coffin, or with the minister's permission, other symbols of the life and faith

of the deceased. In military funerals it is customary for medals awarded to the deceased to be placed on the coffin.

Many parishes surround the coffin with bier lights. These are tall free-standing candlesticks placed beside a coffin once it is positioned at the top of the nave. There may be two, four or six of these candlesticks, according to local custom, set out in pairs around the coffin. It used to be customary for the tall candles used in bier lights to be of unbleached wax, but this custom is now rare. In some churches the Paschal Candle may also be placed alongside the coffin 'in sure and certain hope of the resurrection to eternal life through our Lord Jesus Christ', and the bier lights lit from it during the ceremony. This can be a powerful moment in the ceremony, speaking of the hope of resurrection to those who mourn.

The Gathering

Well before the service commences it is important to ensure that the sound system is switched on and that any radio microphones have charged batteries and are switched to mute. Testing microphones five minutes before a funeral while mourners arrive is unsettling and amateurish. If former colleagues or members of the family are to offer tributes or read a lesson, it is important that the officiating minister – or verger – locates them, explains when and where they are to stand, including instructions about the use of the church's microphones so that there is no embarrassment. If at all possible it is good to get them to come in advance of the rest of the family so that they can experience what it feels like standing at the lectern, looking out at a sea of faces.

Some clergy make the mistake of beginning the service with a list of ten things people are not to do. As far as possible, if there are to be announcements, such as asking people to turn off their mobile phones, it is far better to make them *before* the cortège arrives and the service begins, and to find ways of saying things without being hectoring. Otherwise the congregation is put on edge and we shut down the chances of their participating in the service and hearing anything about the love of God.

There is considerable regional variation in the customs surrounding the reception of a coffin at funerals, and much will depend on the weather. In some communities it is the practice for the extended family – and indeed sometimes the entire congregation – to follow the coffin into church. In other places it is customary for just the immediate family to follow. Some families will prefer to be seated in advance so that they can compose themselves. Whichever option is preferred, it needs to be agreed in advance, particularly if members of the family are to act as bearers. If at all possible it is also a good idea for the minister to meet the coffin either at the roadside or at the door of the church, in order to have a chance to greet the immediate family personally out of earshot of the congregation. Ministers should never assume that a congregation will be familiar with funeral etiquette, and they – or the funeral director – may need to ask the congregation to stand at the entry of the coffin before they recite the opening sentences of Scripture.

As in all acts of worship, the minister sets the tone for the service and it helps if he or she actually looks at the congregation when greeting them. Faces communicate, and eye contact will help bring a congregation together. The pattern for these introductory words in *Common Worship* is only a guide. Ministers need to familiarize themselves with the text and the details of what they want to say so that they are not reading anything verbatim. It is important to put the congregation at its ease by adding words of welcome that are the minister's own and said in a way that is natural and warm, without being effusive. For example, a minister may wish specifically to welcome members of the family, colleagues from work or those who have travelled far to be present at the funeral. If the death took place in difficult circumstances it would be artificial if no reference were made to this. This sort of approach 'softens' the liturgy and engages the attention of the congregation. The officiant can then move directly either into the Prayers of Penitence or the Collect, and/or the opening hymn as appropriate. It is certainly good to have a hymn early on in the proceedings because it enables the congregation 'to arrive' and to settle.

If the funeral is set within the context of the Eucharist, which is the norm in Roman Catholic funerals but unusual in an

Anglican context, there will always be a confession of sin in the liturgy. In a non-eucharistic service, Prayers of Penitence are optional. There are few funerals where there are no feelings of guilt around. There may be feelings of failure on the part of some individuals or relatives, a sense of 'unfinished business' or unresolved disagreements. Children – of any age – can feel they 'let their parents down' in some undefined way or never did enough for them. But what would be 'enough'? The deceased will also have got some things wrong, and this may need to be acknowledged before God in prayer too. Whether it is good to do so liturgically at the outset of the funeral or to include words of penitence and forgiveness later in the service in the context of the intercessions is a matter of pastoral judgement. The value of the former approach is that it includes a declaration of the forgiveness of God in the words of absolution spoken by the priest. The value of the latter is that, embroidered into the flow of other prayers, it may feel more natural and accessible. It also dispels the unhelpful reputation of the Church as preoccupied with guilt and sin.

Readings and Sermon

There must be at least one reading from Scripture, ideally from the New Testament, and in most funerals this is preceded by a psalm (usually Psalm 23), which may be said or sung. If sung this can be in a metrical version such as 'The King of Love my Shepherd is' or 'The Lord's my Shepherd', sung to Crimond. There is merit in sticking with the familiar but equally there is scope for reciting a different psalm, such as Psalm 121 ('I lift up my eyes to the hills') or Psalm 15 ('Lord, who may dwell in your tabernacle?')

If there are two readings the psalm may be sung between the two. Some families may feel more comfortable reading a poem than a portion of Scripture. A selection of possible poems and spiritual readings is included as Appendix E. If this is the preferred option it is all the more important for the minister to choose with care the reading from Scripture and give it due prominence. In some

funerals the reading(s) from the Bible are not listened to because they are read badly. Not everyone knows how to introduce the reading or how to close it, let alone how to pronounce certain words. Some mourners may be nervous and read too quickly; others may be unfamiliar with using a microphone and end up booming. Of course, sometimes the culprit is not the reader at all but the sound system operator who is slow on adjusting the decibel level until the reading is almost over. Ministers may need to weigh up between involving the family but having Scripture read badly or reading it clearly themselves in order to comment upon it.

Common Worship makes provision for a eulogy but not as a substitute for a sermon. The subject of preaching at funerals will be dealt with later. Suffice it to say that if a personal tribute is to be given by a member of the family, a friend or work colleague, it does need to be dovetailed into the structure of the funeral carefully. Above all it should precede rather than follow the minister's address. That way, if the eulogy has suddenly disclosed facts about the deceased that the minister didn't know, or if what has been said has clearly unsettled the congregation, the minister has the opportunity to retrieve the situation.

Prayers

Common Worship provides a framework for prayers of intercession that will always need to be tailored to the occasion. There is no requirement that the minister lead the prayers, and in a church setting it may be good for a different voice to be heard at this point. But if someone other than the officiating minister is leading the prayers it is sensible for the minister and intercessor to liaise with one another more than five minutes before the beginning of the service at the back of the church. Leading a congregation in prayer at a funeral can be far from straightforward, and people deserve support and training to help them do it well. It can be a particular challenge, for example, when there are tensions between different parts of a family. There is also a difference between biddings and intercessions, and the two

should not be confused. Biddings are addressed to the congregation, encouraging them to pray. Intercessions are addressed directly to God. They should never be directed horizontally at a congregation in an attempt to inform them or improve them.

The prayers at a funeral, as in any service, need preparation, and the framework set out in *Common Worship* is to be commended. Prayers need to relate both to the theme of the readings and to the sermon they follow in the service. If responses are to be said they need to be stated clearly at the outset of the prayers and repeated by the congregation. The prayers are fittingly concluded by saying the Lord's Prayer together, and if there is a printed order of service, this should be printed out in full within it. The loss of a common language in worship over the last 40 years has fragmented religious observance, and the most serious casualty has been the loss of an agreed version of the Lord's Prayer. For generations this was a key spiritual text uniting in prayer both regular worshippers of all denominations and those on the fringes of the church. We should never presume that people know the words. If in doubt, it is advisable to stick with the traditional version of the Lord's Prayer. Few things are guaranteed to upset a grieving family more than finding they can't say the one prayer they thought they did know by heart.

Commendation and Farewell

The slot immediately after the sermon or the slot between the prayers and the Commendation and Farewell are good places to have another hymn or piece of music, partly to help the congregation take on board all that has been said. At the end of the hymn the minister should remember to invite the congregation to remain standing for the Commendation. At this point in the service, *Common Worship* specifically and rightly instructs the minister to 'stand by the coffin'. In spite of this directive, many ministers still remain imprisoned in their stalls and underplay the dramatic significance of the moment of commendation. In a soci-

ety in which death is taboo, it seems that the dead have once again become untouchable, not unlike when in the days of Jesus priests and rabbis were subject to rules of ritual purity. Standing beside the coffin, the minister resting a hand upon it in prayerful silence before speaking the words of commendation, is an enormously powerful act. If appropriate, the minister may feel it right to invite members of the immediate family to gather round and join in the ceremony. This is certainly easier to do in a church, where there is likely to be more room, than in a crematorium, gathered around the catafalque.

Common Worship provides authorized words to be spoken by the minister at this point, but also permits the additional use of prayers of entrusting and commending:

> God our creator and redeemer,
> by your power Christ conquered death
> and entered into glory.
> Confident of his victory
> and claiming his promises,
> we entrust N to your mercy
> in the name of Jesus our Lord,
> who died and is alive
> and reigns with you,
> now and for ever. **Amen.** (p. 267)

In this prayer the person is being entrusted to almighty God. What has already happened at the moment of death is now repeated liturgically, as much for the benefit of the bereaved as for the deceased. At the civil funeral of a friend, when the 'service' reached this point in the proceedings the celebrant stood before the coffin and, addressing the deceased by name, said: 'You will always live in our memories.' It was a bleak moment. The contrast with the Christian view of death could not be more pronounced.

During the prayer of commendation or at its conclusion, the minister may sprinkle the coffin with water in remembrance of the person's baptism. At a crematorium the prayer of commendation is immediately followed by the Committal, but in a

church service the minister now leads the coffin and family out of church, either to the graveside for the burial or to the waiting hearse for the journey to the crematorium or local cemetery. Many clergy like to recite the words of Nunc Dimittis as they lead the coffin out of church, or the prayer 'God be in my head' from the sixteenth-century Sarum Primer, with its evocative last line: 'God be at mine end and at my departing'. In some rural areas, where the crematorium is a very long way away, it is not unusual, with the permission of the family, for the funeral director to be asked to conduct the Committal and for the minister, family and congregation to stay behind. In such cases the church door or lychgate really is the point of farewell.

Requiems

The title 'Requiem Eucharist' derives from the Latin *requiem*, meaning 'rest'. It denotes a Eucharist celebrated in memory of a dead person either at their funeral or soon after, or on the annual commemoration of the faithful departed on 2 November (All Souls' Day). Today the word has become dissociated both from a funeral and from a celebration of the Eucharist. In popular usage it is likely to refer to any number of musical pieces that may be performed independently of liturgical commemoration. The term 'requiem' originated with the Latin words of the introit of the service, 'Grant unto them eternal rest'. The theme of rest recurs later in the Eucharist during the breaking of the consecrated bread. In the seventh century the devotional anthem Agnus Dei (Lamb of God) was introduced to accompany the breaking of the bread, and in the eleventh century a variant appeared at requiem masses when the phrase 'grant them eternal rest' was substituted for the words 'grant us peace' in the final petition. In the early Church these prayers for 'rest' were not so much concerned with the repose of the soul after death (as was to become the case in later centuries) as with the hope of Sabbath rest and festivity. Prayer for the dead in the early Church was born of a faith in the resurrection, and a funeral Eucharist should always reflect this.

Common Worship provides the outline and the texts – propers – for a funeral when it takes place in the context of a Eucharist, the Commendation and Farewell taking place after everyone has received Holy Communion and the ablutions are completed. According to local custom, the priest presiding at the Eucharist may wear purple or black vestments, or indeed white vestments in testimony of the resurrection. White will be particularly appropriate in the case of the funeral of a child. Although no longer fashionable, black vestments (which are often embroidered with silver), when combined with white flowers, can combine to make a powerful visual statement of the Christian hope in the face of death, and need not be oppressive.

Paupers' funerals

Under Section 46 of the Public Health (Control of Diseases) Act 1984, every municipality is obliged to make provision for the disposal of dead bodies in their area when there are no known next of kin to take responsibility or the family is unable to pay for it. If there are family or friends, they are at liberty to attend the funeral but they have no say in the arrangements. Since at least the reign of Queen Elizabeth I, under whom the Tudor Poor Laws were codified and differentiation made between the 'deserving' and 'undeserving' poor, these funerals were known as 'Paupers' funerals'. Today they are called less pejoratively 'public health funerals', though the old title is still around.

Typically a simple, but it is hoped dignified, service is held, followed by a cremation or burial in a communal grave. The body is often transported in a van rather than a hearse. In past decades these funerals were mainly of vagrants, but also of elderly, confused patients who died forgotten and unloved in workhouses, geriatric hospitals and asylums. These institutions have long since gone, but some people still die alone and destitute. If no known next of kin comes forward, the council will organize the funeral and pay for it. As this is public money, councils will usually put the work out to tender, with the result that most authorities have a contract with

a local funeral director who undertakes such funerals on behalf of the municipality.

When a local authority organizes the funeral, it will pay for the transport of the coffin to and from the crematorium or cemetery, and for a minister of religion or other celebrant to officiate at the funeral. As the Established Church, it used to be customary, in the absence of the known religion of the deceased, for Anglican clergy to be requested to conduct such funerals, but this is no longer automatically the case. The decision usually rests with the funeral director. Again in the past, burial in a communal grave following a brief service at the graveside was customary. Today cremation is more usual because it is cheaper.

A survey carried out by the Local Government Association found that 2,900 such funerals were conducted in England and Wales in 2011, and the numbers are predicted to rise in step with the ageing population of the nation. Research by the University of Bath's Institute for Policy Research has discovered that a small but growing number of families are turning to these tax-payer-funded 'public health funerals' because they have no alternative. Although the legal provision is intended to be a backstop, and in spite of the stigma attached to such funerals, increasingly some families are driven to seek help because of the escalating cost of funerals. The average cost of a funeral, whether burial or cremation, including the administration of the deceased's estate, now stands at £7,622. This constitutes a rise of 80 per cent since 2004.[4] A debt crisis centre in Plymouth reported that in their area one of the most common reasons that catapults families into debt is meeting the cost of a funeral. They simply had no idea that it could be so expensive, but were ashamed to ask for help, and took out loans at extortionate rates that they then could not repay.

It is always a profound sadness when there is no congregation at a funeral, no one to mourn a person's passing. Good funeral directors will want to co-operate with the clergy in such circumstances, attending the chapel and witnessing the Committal.

---

4 Source of information, *Church Times*, 24 January 2014, p. 8.

Some clergy take it upon themselves to gather a small congregation for such funerals, believing that the Christian community should honour those who had no family. Whether or not anyone is present to form a congregation, and whether or not we know anything about the person who died beyond their name, they are still worthy of respect and should be commended to God with love and prayer. The recitation of Psalm 139 is particularly appropriate on such occasions, with its appeal to the God of our journey who watches us growing in our mother's womb and is 'acquainted with all my ways' (v. 2). On such occasions it may also be good to pray for those who loved and remembered the person in their life, but who appear to have neglected them in their death.

Checklist

Given the variety of permutations that are possible, the following checklist relates only to a funeral in church.

- Ensure that reserved parking signs are set outside the church early on for the hearse and cars carrying the immediate family.
- Ensure the sound system is switched on, that any radio microphones have charged batteries and are switched to mute.
- Reserve sufficient seating at the front of the church for family and immediate mourners, and make sure they are equipped with orders of service. Try to gauge accurate numbers in advance to avoid overestimating the seating required and leaving empty pews behind the immediate family, who then feel exposed.
- Meet the coffin and mourners at the roadside or at the door of the church in order to greet them personally before going into church.
- The coffin is normally placed at the front of the nave, feet facing east. Funeral directors normally come with trestles in two sizes: tall and short. If the custom is to cover the coffin with a pall, tall trestles will be necessary. Otherwise the shorter trestles may be more convenient.
- In addition to flowers and a pall, a Bible or cross may be placed on the coffin, or symbols of the deceased's life, such as military medals.
- In some parishes, by tradition the coffin is surrounded by bier lights. There may be two, four or six of these large freestanding candlesticks, according to custom, set out in pairs.
- In churches that have a Paschal Candle, this may be placed at the foot of the chancel steps or adjacent to the coffin 'in sure and certain hope of the resurrection to eternal life through our Lord Jesus Christ'.
- At the Commendation and Farewell it is good practice for the minister to stand beside the coffin, placing his or her hand on it while speaking. The immediate family may be invited to gather round the coffin at this point. If necessary the bier lights should be moved.

- At the Commendation or at its conclusion, the minister may sprinkle the coffin with holy water, walking around it. If this is customary, have the holy water bucket and aspergillum to hand.
- If a body is to be received in church in advance of the funeral, the minister may elect to sprinkle the coffin at this point. If this is customary, the holy water bucket and aspergillum need to be at hand.
- If the funeral takes place in the context of a Requiem Eucharist, the priest may wear purple, black or white vestments according to local custom.

8

Music

Hope is the ability to hear the music of the future. Faith is the courage to dance to it today.

Peter Kuzmic

Last year I took my aunt's funeral in Somerset. She had been a lifelong communicant, and I discussed with my non-churchgoing cousins what we might sing at her funeral, and watched them panic and reach into their memory of school assemblies. Thank goodness we didn't have to endure 'One more step along the road I go' or I think my old aunt would have turned in her coffin. But it illustrated what clergy the length and breadth of the country know, namely that the Christian culture that has nourished our nation has largely disintegrated and the choice of hymns at funerals is often limited to those learnt at school.

There are few places in society today where we say or sing things together, but church is one of them. Once upon a time performances in theatres and cinemas ended with the audience standing to attention to sing the National Anthem. FA Cup Finals still resound to the words of the hymn 'Abide with Me', and perhaps following the London Olympics this old favourite will make a comeback. Meetings of the Women's Institute often enjoy singing 'Jerusalem', and congregations on Remembrance Sunday may unite in singing 'O God our Help in Ages Past'. But these are exceptions to the rule. For most people today the occasions when they unite with others in word or song, beyond singing 'Happy Birthday' to a member of the family or a colleague at work, are few and far between. It is one of the things that makes church distinctive in the twenty-first century. Put another way, it's what makes church odd. At a funeral today a congregation is more

likely to know the words of Frank Sinatra's song 'I Did It My Way' than the words of the twenty-third psalm.

Hymn singing

Hymnody came late on to the scene in Anglicanism, mainly from the Methodism that it rejected. In contradistinction to Methodism and Lutheranism, where much of Christian doctrine is communicated through hymns, the Church of England has never had any hymnody in common. In the nineteenth century, however, there was an explosion of interest in hymns, as a result of which *Hymns Ancient and Modern* became the nearest thing to being mainstream Church of England, while Anglo-Catholics favoured its rival, the *English Hymnal*. Along with the King James Bible and the Book of Common Prayer, these hymnals were exported to the British Empire and nourished the spirituality of the English-speaking world in times of war, death and tragedy, as well as in times of celebration and festivity.

What distinguished these hymnals and contributed to the distinctive nature of Anglican worship was the commitment of their editors to translate hymns from the ancient and medieval Church and make them available to a new generation of Christians. These treasuries of devotion are no longer so common and, aside from rural communities whose preferences remain more traditional, many of the hymns our grandparents knew and loved are not as widely sung as once they were. The Christian corporate memory is diminishing fast. Traditional hymnody is in decline, some commentators gloomily predicting even the loss of Christmas carols, with 'O Little Town of Bethlehem' losing out to 'Jingle Bells' and 'I'm Dreaming of a White Christmas'. This decline is also impacting funerals. The possibilities for Christian song in the face of struggle and loss, as well as the ability to voice praise for the hope of resurrection or thanksgiving for a much-loved parent at the end of a long and happy life, have contracted. Unless we wake up to the challenge, encouraging more and better singing in our schools, expanding their musical repertoire to re-embrace traditional hymnody, the

next generation will have even fewer spiritual resources to sustain them in the autumn of their lives and with which to express joy to God or handle grief.[1]

Lack of confidence, in combination with unfamiliarity with either the words or a tune, means that many people are simply not singing hymns at funerals. This is particularly the case with men, who are not helped if the hymn is pitched too high for their comfort. Most congregations would not pass muster with John Wesley, who directed his flock to 'sing lustily and with good courage'. Singing is an intensely physical act involving the whole body: belly, lungs, voice, ears and mouth. You can't sing from the neck up. Part of the problem is that our generation has become used to being entertained. As a result we have become passive recipients in worship. We are no longer used to standing up and participating and using our bodies and voices other than in sport. Clergy report that they often find themselves singing a solo at a funeral, belting out the words in a desperate attempt to lead a reluctant congregation. If you've got a decent voice this is feasible, but not all ministers have either the voice or the confidence to be a quasi-cantor. A key task, therefore, for those presiding at funerals is to create the right atmosphere not only for unchurched people to relax but one that is sufficiently contagious for them to want to stand up and join in.

In the run-up to a funeral some clergy provide the bereaved with a booklet of 20 or so popular hymns to look through. This can be particularly helpful to a non-churchgoing family who may feel anxious about being put on the spot by the vicar. Not only does it shield them from embarrassment when their poor knowledge of the repertoire of church music is exposed, it genuinely gives them leisure to reflect and identify what is going to work best for them. There is comfort in the familiar, and singing hymns remembered from childhood, even if it is only 'All Things Bright and Beautiful', can be a good counterbalance to the pressure to create something unique for a funeral. It is preferable to put the full text of hymns

---

1 See the excellent study by Anne Harrison (2009), *Recovering the Lord's Song: Getting Sung Scripture Back into Worship*, Cambridge: Grove.

into their hands rather than just give a list of first lines, which may not ring any bells. Better still if there is a CD with recordings of the hymns so that they can listen to them at home. Failing that, one can access almost any hymn online these days. Many sites will play hymns through, though they don't necessarily use familiar tunes, and sometimes it's the tune that sits in the memory and is the evocative thing, rather than the words. A sample shortlist of popular funeral hymns is included as Appendix C.

In conversation with bereaved families it is not unusual for them to say that they don't want to sing anything too gloomy or depressing. 'Abide with Me' often falls into this category. The desire for something bright and uplifting, such as 'Lord of All Hopefulness' or 'Guide Me, O Thou Great Redeemer', is to be welcomed, and hymns of the resurrection are always suitable at a Christian funeral. However, in terms of overall musical balance, sad or melancholy hymns should not automatically be excluded. They have the ability to evoke and release grief. They give us permission to be sad, and this leads to the place of lament in Christian worship.

The place of lament

The psalms are full of laments: songs that express loss whether of health, power, friendship, life or even of a sense of the presence of God. We do not know the original melodies to which these ancient Hebrew songs were sung or the musical instruments that accompanied them. All we know is that these texts in the Bible carry the superscription 'lament', together with directions to the temple musicians about the choice of tune to be sung. Laments form the musical score in the spirituality of pain and bewilderment. Through a combination of words and music, the anguish that comes with loss is expressed without denial or diminution. Laments enable us to be emotionally honest before God. They enable us to discover not only what we do feel but what we *should* feel. They distil feeling, shape it and to a degree purify it. It is part of the way God heals the human heart and enables us to move towards the fullness of joy that he wills for all people.

It is widely said that as a culture we no longer know how to lament. We have lost both the language and the music of grief. As a result, impromptu wayside shrines where someone was killed in a car crash, flowers left on the pavement outside a house, teddy bears by the school gates or candles burning in jam-jars have become the main ways we express solidarity with those who grieve. There is nothing the matter with any of these things, but they are unlikely to reach deep into the heart of grief. If as a society we do not constantly and consistently practise the art of recognizing, accepting and expressing loss and sadness, we will never cultivate the capacity to deal with tragedy when its shadow falls across a community.

It is salutary to note how rarely sacred music features in our attempts to grapple with loss. In the film *Love Actually* the coffin of a young mother is carried out of church to the sound of the 1970s hit single by the Bay City Rollers, 'Bye, Bye Baby, Baby Goodbye'. The bizarre choice of music and its sheer incongruity makes you laugh, but what is good about the scene is the positive way it portrays the church's ministry. The funeral is clearly taking place in a church, presided over by an Anglican priest. There is nothing stuffy or impersonal about it. Here is the Christian Church going with a choice of popular music that speaks to a grieving congregation mourning a young mother's death. What the scene also confirms is how rare traditional lament is, even in a Christian context.

Reflecting on this state of affairs we need to do two things in parallel. We need to renew our confidence in metrical psalms, traditional hymnody and the rich musical traditions of Christianity, including that of lament. We also need to explore how various forms of music from Bach to Gershwin, from blues to recitative, can help us express grief. These two approaches are not alternatives; we need both. We also need the expertise of first-class Christian musicians to help in the venture, and clergy need to be willing and eager to collaborate with them.[2]

---

2 See Jeremy S. Begbie (2007), *Resounding Truth: Christian Wisdom in the World of Music*, Grand Rapids, MI: Baker Academic. I am particularly indebted to Professor Begbie's stimulating lecture on the place of lament today, delivered to the Chester Diocesan Conference in 2013.

Recorded music

There will always be a debate about the merits or demerits of recorded music at funerals, whether the service is held in a church or entirely at a crematorium. Some clergy refuse point-blank to countenance the idea and most musicians loathe the artificiality of canned music. Without doubt a sensitive organist and well-trained choir will support and encourage congregational participation without dominating. As a result people who otherwise would be shy about singing don't feel so exposed and are prepared to try. A soloist can similarly lift an act of worship and be truly inspiring. But choirs and soloists are hard to come by in many areas, particularly at short notice, and few families' budgets extend to hiring a quartet of professional singers. For these reasons churches equipped with modern technology and a decent sound system may opt to encourage congregational participation by the sensitive use of pre-recorded hymn singing. In the absence of anything else, this may be the best option, though even the best modern technology will still be dependent on someone who is competent at the back of church pressing the correct buttons at the appropriate moment and playing the right track.

One unfortunate disadvantage of having a service in church followed by a Committal at the crematorium occurs when a family is charged twice over for an organist: once for the organist at church, and a second time for the organist at the crematorium, even though the person there may play very little indeed. For families operating on a tight budget, having the entire funeral at the crematorium then becomes the cheaper option. Are we disadvantaging the poor? It is certainly impacting on our mission.

Churches with good sound systems can offer a bereaved family flexibility in the choice of music beyond the canon of sacred music, something that is taken for granted in crematoria. Accessible classical music usually receives a fairer wind from clergy than pop music. Clergy often undervalue the extent to which contemporary songs can be incredibly important in many people's lives. The rendition of 'You Raise Me Up' at George Best's funeral was a case in point. It profoundly expressed the degree and depth of

inspiration that the footballer brought to those who had watched him play in his heyday.

A pause for reflection during a long wordy service, perhaps following an address or eulogy, can be helped by a sensitive choice of music. It can relieve tension without detracting from the flow of the service and be a real help to mourners. I remember attending the funeral of a friend who had lived all her life by the sea. As we sat in the Cornish church, the wind blowing a gale and the sea raging, just before we stood for the Commendation, over the speakers was played one of Britten's Sea Interludes from his opera *Peter Grimes*. Equally moving was the mellow jazz played at the end of the cremation of a family friend. Following the closing prayers his favourite piece by Oscar Peterson perfectly encapsulated his joyful laissez-faire approach to life. There are times when music goes deeper than words, and we discover emotions we didn't know we had.

Music choices for funerals are certainly becoming more eclectic, if not bizarre. According to a survey compiled by funeral directors in the UK and USA, only 25 per cent of songs requested at funerals are hymns, and only 4 per cent are pieces of classical music.[3] Included in the funeral top 20 songs, after Frank Sinatra's 'I Did It My Way', which comes top of the pops, are Sarah Brightman/Andrea Bocelli, 'Time to Say Goodbye'; Robbie Williams, 'Angels'; Judy Garland, 'Somewhere Over the Rainbow'; Westlife, 'You Raised Me Up'; Gerry and the Pacemakers, 'You'll Never Walk Alone'; and amazingly, Monty Python, 'Always Look on the Bright Side of Life'. In Australia their favourite two songs are Barbra Streisand's 'Memories' and Mariah Carey's 'Hero'. Meanwhile at funerals in Germany their favourite two songs are Avril Lavigne's 'When You're Gone' and Enya's 'Only Time'.

A survey conducted by the Royal School of Church Music (RSCM)[4] produced requests for music from *Star Wars*, *Doctor*

---

3 Charles Saatchi, 'What Songs Have You Selected for Your Funeral?' *London Evening Standard*, 21 November 2013.

4 The survey was conducted by Stuart Robinson as reported by *Church Times*, 26 April 2013.

Who and even Johnny Cash's 1963 hit, 'Ring of Fire' at one crema-tion. John Lennon's song 'Imagine' is a frequent request, though one usually rejected by ministers for its 'theological dissonance'. It is not clear how scientific any of these surveys are, but it does confirm that a change in musical taste for funerals is not unique to the UK. It also reveals how pervasive English pop culture now is the world over and how difficult it is to reconnect the current generation with the riches of traditional Christian hymnody. Many bereaved people, no longer familiar with most hymns, fear to voice their preferred choice of music lest it be scorned by the vicar. As a result they opt for a 'non-religious' funeral conducted by a civil celebrant because it is easier.

How we handle music requests is never going to be easy or straightforward. Clergy will have an instinctive 'feel' for what will work and what may jar. As with 'Imagine', some pop music is simply not suitable – at least not in the context of a Christian funeral. But in the end, generosity in the choice of music is more likely to win us friends than what may be perceived as cultural snobbishness. The Church of England will die of good taste. We need to draw people through a wider choice of music, not alien-ate them.

9

Preaching into grief

For I am not ashamed of the gospel.

Romans 1.16

Some say that the age of sermons is past. They see the sermon as a relic of a bygone era and irrelevant to the contemporary life of faith. It is certainly true that compared with our grandparents' generation our attention span is not as long. We find it difficult to sit still and listen to someone speaking. In my experience, however, far from not wanting an address, the bereaved are desperate for someone to speak into their grief. They long for someone to name their feelings and to shape their experience, particularly when their loss is devastating. They long for someone who has the confidence to ask legitimate questions of God in the face of suffering and above all to give them hope in the face of death. Far from being uninterested, the bereaved are uniquely receptive to what a minister has to say.

A well-planned funeral service will include the sharing of memories and give expression to the variety of feelings that may be present in the church or crematorium chapel. There is likely to be a mixture of love, grief, anger, guilt and respect in the assembled congregation. This needs to be acknowledged by the minister in an appropriate way, if not in the address then at least in how the service is introduced and the congregation welcomed, or during the course of the prayers. If this is not done properly, a sense of unreality can descend on the proceedings. There must always be adequate room in a funeral service for sadness, brokenness and questioning.

Tributes and eulogies

These days a funeral service cannot afford to be impersonal. It must include a fitting tribute to the deceased in the belief that every person is precious to God. Often this is best done separately by a member of the family, a family friend or colleague from work, or if time permits by a succession of people. It will be more personal and meaningful than anything a minister could manage. Most people are understandably anxious about speaking in public, particularly on such an occasion, and they may need encouragement. But with a script and the reassurance that it's fine to pause to gather your emotions as necessary, most manage really well. Afterwards they are invariably glad to have made a significant contribution to the service and have a real sense of achievement.

Tributes do need to be scripted. Clergy are used to speaking in public; most people are not. Faced with a large gathering, overcome with the solemnity of the occasion, people easily lose their way, become repetitive and waffle or simply break down. Not only can this be embarrassing for all concerned, but if the funeral is taking place in a crematorium within a fixed time-slot the service is likely to overrun and the funeral director and crematorium staff become anxious. Giving a family a word limit sometimes helps. For example, 600 words takes roughly four to five minutes to deliver. Ideally the minister needs to see the script(s) beforehand so that there are no surprises and to ensure that he or she does not repeat in the sermon what has already been said. But this is not always possible. If the family feel unable to speak or are unwilling to do so, it will fall to the minister to gather as much information and insight into the deceased's life as possible and to incorporate the material into her or his address.

Some family members may wish to offer a tribute to the deceased, but not by giving a formal eulogy. They may wish to offer a reading or a poem, and perhaps preface the reading by a few comments of their own. The brave may wish to sing. In such cases the minister needs to orchestrate the proceedings carefully, making sure that his or her own address comes last.

It is not unknown for a family tribute to hijack a service! The word 'eulogy' literally means 'good words'. Sometimes that is fine, but a panoply of undiluted praise often sounds a false note and is unreal. The best tributes acknowledge that we all have feet of clay. In Oliver Cromwell's immortal phrase, 'Paint me warts and all.'

But what if the deceased was loathed? I recall the first burial I ever took as a young curate. Gazing down into the grave at her husband's coffin six feet below, the widow looked up and said, 'Well, all I can say is, good riddance to the old ******'. The rest of the sentence is unprintable. None of the anger that erupted at the graveside had been voiced during my pre-funeral visit to the family, and I was taken aback by the vehemence of her outpouring. We expect eulogies to be full of 'good words' but sometimes there are few or no good words to be said at all. A person may have been despised or hated for a variety of reasons, and in such situations no guidelines can assist the minister tasked with presiding at the funeral. The hope is that any underlying anger or frustration will have surfaced long before the funeral, perhaps during the initial funeral visit or when viewing the body. But sometimes, as happened to me, things can be so tightly wrapped up that there are no clues and then an explosion of rage occurs.

Years of ministry among the bereaved should hone a minister's intuition. Presiding at a funeral one can occasionally sense underlying tension in a congregation that needs to be released in some way. Sometimes the formality of the liturgy comes to the rescue, providing words that can bear the weight of anger or disgust. Silence for reflection, carefully crafted Prayers of Penitence and praying the Our Father itself, at the heart of which stands a covenant of forgiveness, can all help in this regard. Whatever one's personal opinions about the deceased – and it is important to remember that the dead cannot reply to their accusers – we should not lose sight of the mercy of God 'to whom all hearts are open and from whom no secrets are hidden'. Jesus came to call 'not the righteous but sinners' (Mark 2.17), and we all stand in need of forgiveness.

In sure and certain hope

It is good to look back and give thanks for a person's life, but a Christian funeral worthy of the name needs to be more than that. It needs to be evangelistic in the sense that we are shaping what we say by reference to our faith in Jesus Christ. For example, it needs to include an acknowledgement of the finality of death – not in an oppressive way but 'in sure and certain hope of the resurrection to eternal life'. Our belief in the God who brings light out of darkness and life out of death lies at the heart of the Christian gospel and needs to permeate both what we say and the way we say it. It is why a family tribute is not an alternative to a sermon. People nowadays are increasingly uncertain about any form of resurrection life beyond death and ministers should have more confidence in speaking of God and of his love for us in Jesus Christ. Sharing our convictions about the glory of our risen life in Christ both now and after death is not being arrogant. Being confident and being pastorally sensitive are not mutually exclusive.

Unfortunately what sometimes passes for Christian belief in resurrection life can become subtly skewed. We see it, for example, in the profoundly sub-Christian reading extracted and taken out of context from a sermon once preached in St Paul's Cathedral by Henry Scott Holland, and now popular at funerals and memorial services: 'Death is nothing at all. It does not count. I have only slipped away into the next room.' Whatever death is, it is not 'nothing at all'. The biblical writers will have none of this pretence. Death is not to be dismissed lightly. Indeed Saint Paul describes death as 'the last enemy' (1 Cor. 15.26). Death stands in opposition to God the creator, redeemer and sustainer of all. It is why the Bible is honest about grief, as in the case of Mary Magdalene, who sobs beside the empty tomb on Easter morning. It is why Paul, when writing to the church in Thessalonica, insists that it is not wrong to grieve, only that we should not 'grieve as others do who have no hope' (1 Thess. 4.13). It is important to grasp this point because in the current culture of 'thanksgiving services' people often need to be given permission to grieve.

If we have sometimes subtly skewed the Christian attitude to death, some have distorted the resurrection of Christ, as though it were little more than the resuscitation of a corpse or as though the dead body of Jesus came back to life just as it was before he was crucified. This can impact the way we talk at funerals because we then fall into the trap of talking about dead bodies as if they were discarded shells. Bodies matter. The Gospels collectively witness to the profound change that occurred in the body of the resurrected Christ, and that transformation is our destiny too. Another trap is to spiritualize the resurrection and to speak of the risen Lord as if he were no more than a ghost. Paul is clear about the transformed nature of Christ's resurrected body: 'So it is with the resurrection of the dead. What is sown is perishable, what is raised is imperishable. It is sown in dishonour, it is raised in glory. It is sown in weakness, it is raised in power. It is sown a physical body, it is raised a spiritual body' (1 Cor. 15.42–44). We make sense of our death by seeing it in relation to Jesus' death and resurrection.

The message of Easter is that death is final and death is real. There is both continuity *and* change. In the resurrection of Christ, God initiates a new creation. All things are being made new and God invites us to share in this new creation. Death is both an end *and* a new beginning. For this reason, as we face death, either our own or the death of those nearest and dearest to us, there is nothing to fear. The future is in God's hands. In this understanding, death represents a pattern of change, not destruction. We are going home to God. This is the hope we are called upon to share with the bereaved.

If the average minister conducts 25 funerals a year with, say, 50 mourners present at each funeral, this adds up to an impressive congregation well in excess of 1,000 people by the time a year ends, most of whom are unlikely to have darkened the door of a church. Seen in this light we should not underestimate the opportunity funerals represent to proclaim the Christian faith. If appropriate it is good to encourage a congregation to revisit their faith or pick it up again if they had discarded it. Immanuel Kant, the great German philosopher, said that there are only

three questions in life worth spending time on: What can I know? What ought I to do? What may I hope? It is the third of these questions a preacher at a Christian funeral is called upon to explore. It is hope, not just empathy, that should characterize our preaching; and with the evidence of our mortality before us, we should not delay in laying hold of it.

Burials

Give rest, O Christ, to thy servants with thy saints,
where sorrow and pain are no more,
neither sighing, but life everlasting.

Thou only art immortal, the creator and maker of all:
and we are mortal, formed from the dust of the earth,
and unto earth shall we return.
For so thou didst ordain when thou createdst me, saying,
'Dust thou art, and unto dust shalt thou return.'
All we go down to the dust;
and weeping o'er the grave we make our song:
Alleluia, alleluia, alleluia.

Give rest, O Christ, to thy servants with thy saints,
where sorrow and pain are no more,
neither sighing, but life everlasting.

Russian *Kontakion* for the Dead

'Earth to earth; ashes to ashes; dust to dust.' These ancient words
from the burial service echo through the pages of English literature. There is something wonderfully natural about a traditional
English burial in a country churchyard. With the service in church
over, the family and congregation follow the vicar and the coffin
outside and gather round the grave for the interment. Some rural
churches still boast their own parish bier – the pallet or trolley
on which a coffin is transported to and from the church and then
finally to the graveside. Most burials today, however, are not so
bucolic. Following the service in church there is more often than

not a second journey in the funeral director's cars either to the overflow cemetery outside the town or to a large municipal cemetery owned by the local borough.

On arriving at the cemetery it is important for the minister to discover either from the funeral director or from the gravedigger exactly where the grave is, the best path to it and the orientation of the grave so that he or she can stand at its head. Old clerical hands will not be wearing their best cassock or their best black leather shoes, particularly if the ground is sodden, unless they want to end up caked in mud. In winter they will also invest in a warm clerical cloak. Rain is by far the worst thing to have to contend with, but with luck a good undertaker will come armed with a stash of umbrellas.

Once the coffin has been taken out of the hearse and raised on to the bearers' shoulders, the minister should lead the coffin and mourners to the grave, usually guided by the gravedigger. It is customary for the procession to proceed in silence, but there is no reason why a minister should not recite a psalm or Nunc Dimittis if it seems fitting. Beware the fake green grass gravediggers place around a grave. It may look solid and stable but it is likely to be covering uneven muddy ground plus the occasional pothole. It is not unknown for a distracted parson to lose his footing and take a tumble. If the grave is in unconsecrated ground it will be necessary first for the minister to bless the grave on arriving at the graveside before proceeding to the Committal. The prayer for this is printed below on p. 106.

The Committal

By custom at the graveside the minister stands at the head rather than the foot of the coffin, but this may not always be practicable. In most situations the family will be hesitant and not know what to do. They will be grateful to have guidance from the minister and will value the reassurance of lots of eye contact and the odd helping hand. Bearers will similarly take their cue from the minister,

not least because every minister tends to do things slightly differently. So the minister needs to act confidently and give clear directions. Upon arriving at the grave the bearers will lower the coffin from their shoulders and place it initially at the side of the grave, usually on two wooden boards. They will remove any floral tributes tied to the coffin lid and put them on one side. Later, when the grave is filled in, the flowers and wreaths will be laid on the mound of earth. The bearers will then thread lowering straps or webbing around the coffin and through its handles in readiness for positioning it over the grave. While all this is going on, the minister needs to be beckoning to the mourners and inviting them to assemble around the grave as best they can. It is important not to begin the Committal until all are present and everyone can see what is going on.

Common Worship provides two alternative preambles to the act of Committal. The first is a recitation by the minister of verses from Psalm 103 beginning, 'The Lord is full of compassion and mercy'. The second preamble is a contemporary version of the words used in the Book of Common Prayer, itself a translation of the medieval text *Media vita*: 'In the midst of life we are in death'. Ministers will select whichever text is better suited to the occasion. Some clergy like undertakers to lower the coffin into the grave while the preamble to the prayer of Committal is being said and for them then to stand back. Others prefer the bearers to lower the coffin before anything is said and then withdraw, leaving the family gathered around the grave with the officiating minister. In either case the undertaker will wait until the minister gives the nod before directing the bearers to lower the coffin into the grave. As soon as the bearers have withdrawn the minister will need once again to invite the mourners to gather round.

By custom, during the prayer of Committal, as the priest recites the words 'earth to earth; ashes to ashes; dust to dust', soil is thrown on to the coffin below. Normally the undertaker will do this on behalf of the priest, ideally using dry soil rather than clods of earth that thud on the coffin lid below, but it is good to double-check this with the funeral director beforehand. Casting earth on

the coffin is a powerful and poignant moment in the burial rite that brings home the finality of death like nothing else.

Where the body is deposited in a vault, mausoleum or brick grave, *Common Worship* provides different words for the Committal:

We have entrusted our *brother/sister* N to God's mercy,
and now we commit *his/her* body to its resting place. (p. 292)

The burial service concludes with prayers of the minister's choosing and the dismissal. After a suitable interval the minister should withdraw and allow the mourners to pay their own respects in private before greeting them individually. Some mourners may like to throw earth on to the coffin themselves. I know one priest who always has a pack of wet-wipes within easy reach at interments precisely for this reason. The opportunity to clean up afterwards often helps relatives to feel able to throw earth. Other mourners may choose to cast flowers or petals. African and Caribbean families are likely to want to backfill the grave rather than leave it to the official gravedigger. If this is likely to happen the minister would do well to decide, with the family and the funeral director, in advance the transport arrangements back from the cemetery. Otherwise the minister could be stuck at the cemetery for a very long time!

Green funerals

Permission needs to be obtained from the local authority for any burial that is not in a cemetery or churchyard. With permission you can be buried under the apple tree in your back garden, though it is likely to reduce the value of your house! Recent decades have witnessed a surge of interest in protecting the environment, and the popularity of green burial sites is one example of today's heightened ecological awareness. The first woodland burial site was opened in Cumbria in 1991. According to the Natural Death Centre, there are now well over 200 registered natural burial sites in the UK, and new ones are opened every year. The Centre

runs the Association of Natural Burial Grounds, an organization that promotes and sets the standard for environmentally friendly cemeteries. Having a green burial, rather than being cremated, is one last way a person can reduce the carbon footprint each of us makes during our lifetime. In spite of the increasing popularity of these sites, green burials still only account for a small proportion of the funerals that take place nationally.

Contrary to what most people assume, there is no requirement in law to be buried in a coffin. The law simply specifies that as a minimum the body must be clothed from top to toe in a shroud and not be visible to the naked eye. In natural or woodland sites bodies are usually interred in biodegradable coffins made of wicker or cardboard. No gravestones or memorials are erected, but relatives may choose to sponsor the planting of a tree in memory of the deceased or make donations to, for example, an eco-friendly charity. There is no reason why a green burial should not be accompanied by Christian prayer using the authorized formularies of the Church of England, or why it should not be preceded by a funeral service in church in the normal way. Indeed given the failure of the Church in the nineteenth century to engage with the movement to revive cremation, it would be a mistake if it were now to retreat from engaging with this environmentally friendly movement. Canon Law simply requires that if a burial is to take place in unconsecrated ground (which these natural burial grounds are), then the grave must be blessed on the minister's first coming to it if the rites of the Church of England are to be used. *Common Worship* provides the following prayer for this:

O God,
whose Son Jesus Christ was laid in a tomb:
bless, we pray, this grave
as the place where the body of N your servant
   may rest in peace,
through your Son, who is the resurrection and the life;
who died and is alive and reigns with you
now and for ever. **Amen.** (p. 296)

Graves and graveyards

A grave, as the final place of parting, occupies a unique place in human psychology the world over, to which Mary Magdalene's pilgrimage to the tomb on Easter Day bears ample witness. According to Andrew Marvell, one of our finest metaphysical poets, the grave is 'a fine and private place'.[1] But it is also a public place where individuals, families and communities seek solace in their grief. Perhaps inevitably it is also a place of superstition and fear.

Martin of Tours, one of the best-loved saints and the first Christian who was not a martyr to be publicly commemorated by the Church, died in the year 397. Initially he was buried just outside Tours in France in a humble grave but a generation later his relics were translated to a new resting place inside the city, where they remain to this day. The following words were inscribed on his tomb:

Hic conditus est sanctae memoriae Martinus episcopus
Cuius anima in manu Dei est, sed his totus est
Praesens manifestus omni gratia virtutum.

(Here lies Martin the bishop, of holy memory,
whose soul is in the hand of God; but he is fully here
present and made plain in miracles of every kind.)[2]

The saint may have been in heaven but to the people of Tours he was very much 'present' at his tomb on earth. Moreover his power and mercy were readily available to the faithful gathered there. In many people's minds still, the tomb is a place where it is believed earth and heaven meet in the person of the dead. In the case of saints, as church history reveals, their presence was believed to be made plain by some manifestation of supernatural

---

1 Andrew Marvell, from 'To his Coy Mistress'.
2 E. Le Blant, *Les Inscriptions chrétiennes de la Gaule*, Paris, 1856, i. 240.

power; by a wonderful happening or healing. This belief became the engine of the cult of the saints and of Christian pilgrimage in medieval Europe. Nowadays most Christians, while honouring the grave, would be alert to superstition, though even in the twenty-first century it is perfectly possible for intelligent, rational and indeed sceptical people to hold a clutch of sub-Christian beliefs about the presence of their friends and relatives in a grave. I know one man, an avowed atheist, who regularly goes to the local churchyard where his son is buried and talks to him, ritually kissing his gravestone as he returns home. Nor should we be surprised at such things. Few of us are consistent in our beliefs and practices.

Cemeteries and graveyards are rightly subject to the regulation of Church and state. Cemeteries are owned and maintained either by private companies or by the local authority. Although not owned by the Church of England, for historical reasons the vast majority of such cemeteries have at least a section that has been consecrated by an Anglican bishop. Some municipal cemeteries may have a separate area for Roman Catholics or designated areas for the burial of Jews and Muslims, and these areas will be additionally regulated by their own religious bodies. Churchyards are under the care of the local Parish Church and their maintenance is the responsibility of the PCC, unless they are closed, in which case maintenance is usually transferred to the local authority. Even so much of the day-to-day care of a churchyard will still devolve upon the local church.

The law grants rights of free access to a churchyard, assuming it is not closed to new interments, for the burial of any parishioner or anyone who dies within the bounds of the parish, regardless of their religious affiliation or lack of it. There is no obligation in law for the deceased to be buried 'according to the rites and ceremonies of the Established Church', but people attending the funeral in the churchyard and those officiating at it must still behave 'in a decent and orderly manner'. In unconsecrated land within public burial grounds, ceremonies of any religion or none are allowed under the provisions of the Race Relations Act (1976).

It is the responsibility of the incumbent to maintain meticulously a plan of the churchyard, including the location of graves and how many bodies are buried in each plot. It is also the incumbent's responsibility to ensure that any memorials that are erected in the churchyard meet the specifications laid out in the Diocesan Chancellor's regulations for churchyards. Guidelines vary from diocese to diocese, partly because they need to respond to local traditions, but they are usually concerned with practical matters – especially health and safety issues – and aesthetic sensibilities. For example, the need to keep churchyards tidy and mown mean that it is unusual to allow kerb stones around a grave or for a grave to be covered in stone chippings. Aesthetic concerns tend to focus around the use of appropriate materials, particularly where a grave is close to a medieval church built of local stone. It is why guidelines will often prohibit the erection of polished granite headstones.

Churchyards are both a blessing and a burden, as any parish priest will testify. When families have been recently bereaved they can have very passionate and strong feelings about the sort of memorial stone and inscription they want, both of which in some circumstances can be totally inappropriate. Careful pastoral care of the bereaved and the use of some well-thought-out processes will minimize problems. For this reason it may be helpful to leave a copy of the memorial guidelines with the family when they are visited before the funeral. It is certainly good practice to display the regulations publicly and prominently on a noticeboard in the church porch or churchyard so that no one can claim ignorance.

Clergy are also well advised to ensure that local undertakers, who will talk to the family about the headstone and probably arrange for its erection, are fully aware of memorial guidelines. In this as in other aspects of funeral ministry, we need funeral directors on our side. The soil over a grave takes a long time to settle and if a memorial is installed too soon it may become unstable. Families should be advised to wait for at least 6 and preferably 12 months before installing a memorial. This also gives time for the raw grief of bereaved relatives to subside. By then they are

likely to be more objective about the deceased and about what it is and is not appropriate to write on a headstone. Many dioceses issue application forms to apply for the erection of a headstone in a churchyard, and it is best if the family has to approach the incumbent or parish administrator directly for these forms, rather than via the funeral director. This creates a further opportunity for pastoral contact. It also means that unreasonable requests can be sensitively dealt with straight away.

In these days when care of the environment is high in the national consciousness, many PCCs, particularly in urban areas, see their churchyard as an oasis of wildlife to be treasured and protected. A churchyard can certainly become an educational resource to a parish, encouraging local school children to visit and explore not only the wildlife and the inscriptions on gravestones but the church building itself, with all the opportunities that this presents in witnessing to the gospel. Long live the wilderness! But as Philip Martin points out, one person's wildflower meadow is another person's 'disrespectful mess'.[3] If a PCC resolves to create a haven for wildlife, it would do well to advertise the fact on the church noticeboard and in the local press so that the 'mess' is explained, particularly if distant relatives turn up seeking a grave. And even if this is the policy of the PCC, mowing the grass in the vicinity of the church and along church paths and creating some semblance of order will still be important if the church isn't to look decidedly 'gothic' and unkempt.

Most parishes with a burial ground, be it open or closed, maintain a team of volunteers who give their time and expertise to keep the place tidy and in order. In rural areas it pays to forge a partnership with the local Parish Council, who may be favourably disposed to helping in its maintenance, either practically or by giving grants towards items of capital expenditure such as hedge trimmers or a new mower, or even by paying a contractor to repair frost-damaged paths. It is good for the home team to take a broad view of their work because it is likely to have a pastoral

---

3 Philip Martin, 'Don't Let the Graves Trip You Up', *Church Times*, 1 November 2013, p. 13.

dimension and not be just about grounds maintenance. In most churchyards, particularly at weekends, Christmas and Easter and on special days such as Mothering Sunday, it is not unusual to find mourners weeding their relative's grave or leaving flowers in their memory. Opening up a conversation with them, or even kneeling down and helping them with the weeding, can be a real gift.

11

Cremations

Lord, you have been our refuge
from one generation to another.
Before the mountains were brought forth,
or the earth and the world were formed,
from everlasting to everlasting you are God.
You turn us back to dust and say:
'Turn back, O children of earth.'

Psalm 90.1–3

After a millennium and a half of Christian burial, the revival
of the practice of cremation in the late nineteenth century as a
way of disposing of the dead marked a huge social and religious
change, if not a revolution. The cities of Victorian Britain with
their crowded populations had gradually filled the parish churchyards to overflowing with their dead. This had often resulted in
unhygienic conditions and irreverence, which on occasion had
erupted into public scandal. Initially the crisis was alleviated by
the opening of new municipal cemeteries on the outskirts of the
new industrial towns and cities. The opening of these cemeteries,
however necessary and desirable, had the unfortunate side effect
of weakening the link between church and community. As we
have noted,[1] the churchyard had linked the disposal of the dead
with the living worshipping community of the church, and this
had forged a unique sense of belonging. In urban Britain this link
was now irreversibly weakened and the revival of the practice of
cremation weakened it still further.

---

1 See above, pp. 7–8.

Cremation had begun to be publicly advocated in the 1870s, promoted in part by Victorian ideas of science and technology. Pressure increased following the publication of an article by Sir Henry Thompson in *The Contemporary Review*, and 1875 saw the formation of the Cremation Society. Legal doubts were finally settled by Sir James Stephen's judgement in 1884, and the first crematoria were opened.[2] Cremation won only slow acceptance. The Church was suspicious of the innovation. Many Christians saw it as the revival of a pagan practice and openly opposed it. Some, and not just the theologically conservative, found it difficult to reconcile the practice with their belief in the resurrection of the body.

The combination of suspicion and hostility meant that the Church tended to be remote from the development. As a consequence the architecture, design and symbolism of crematoria were shaped outside a Christian frame of reference, even though some Christian symbolism might be incorporated into the building. In the words of Geoffrey Rowell, 'Cremation, in this country, is basically a secular arrangement to which religion has become attached, and the buildings reflect this ambiguity.'[3] Paradoxically, some of the early crematoria were designed to resemble churches, their chimneys disguised in fake bell-turrets or pseudo-gothic towers to reassure an uncertain public. The architecture of more recent crematoria, however, mirroring contemporary Scandinavian design, tends to be decidedly secular in appearance, though often they are still built on the loggia principle, even with cloisters, their walls adorned with memorial plaques to those who have been cremated.

In the 1960s the balance between burial and cremation shifted dramatically in favour of cremation. In 1963 the Roman Catholic Church changed its stance on cremation and formally granted

2 Douglas J. Davies (2002), *Death, Ritual and Belief*, London and New York: Continuum, p. 231.

3 Geoffrey Rowell (1977), *The Liturgy of Christian Burial*, London: SPCK/Alcuin Club, p. 113.

permission for Catholics to be cremated, though burial remained the preferred option. The watershed year was 1967, when the number of cremations equalled the number of burials.[4] Since then the popularity of cremation has increased year on year and overtaken the number of burials, matched by a corresponding rise in the number of crematoria.

The purpose of cremation is to reduce the corpse to ashes. Unlike burial, however, where the mourners gather round the grave and witness the interment, the actual act of burning is seldom witnessed. In India, in accordance with Hindu custom, the act of cremation is a solemn and public act – the pyre is built and maintained by the grieving family. In Britain, following a funeral service in a church or crematorium chapel, or following a non-religious ceremony, the actual act of cremation takes place privately, 'behind the scenes'. In the words of Douglas Davies, cremation is 'a socially invisible act'.[5] As he points out, the only indication that a cremation is occurring is the visual clue of smoke escaping from the crematorium chimney or the smell of burning, both of which are regarded as socially unacceptable. Modern crematorium technology and European legislation aim to eliminate both things as far as possible. Desirable though such improvements might be, they mask the fact of fire and the reality of death in a way that a burial does not.

In spite of the popularity of cremation, families may still seek reassurance or indeed an explanation of the processes involved at a crematorium. For example, the minister may need to explain to them that although the coffin does not go straight into the flames once it disappears from view at the Committal, the system 'behind the scenes' by which a coffin is placed in a cremator is both efficient and dignified. In the UK the Code of Cremation Practice forbids the opening of a coffin or the removal of the body once it has arrived at a crematorium; so a coffin has to be made of easily combustible material. On average it takes between two and two and a half hours for a human body to be

---

4 Davies, *Death.Ritual and Belief*, p. 28.
5 Davies, *Death.Ritual and Belief*, p. 28..

cremated. A cremator is not designed to cremate more than one body at a time and the bereaved can be assured that corpses are tracked carefully to ensure that the cremated remains they later receive are indeed those of their loved one and not of someone else!

The Committal

The Committal is the final and decisive farewell to the departed and as such constitutes the climax of the funeral service. It is one of the strong moments in a service, for which the church provides authorized words that need to be spoken with clarity and dignity. If the congregation is seated they need to be invited to stand 'for the Committal'. It is good to say this straightforwardly so that the congregation knows what is about to happen and is not taken by surprise. Clergy are familiar with the format of a service but many, perhaps most, of the congregation will not be. There will always be pressure from the staff at a crematorium to keep a service moving and not to overrun its allotted time. This is entirely understandable. Nevertheless it is vital that the Committal should not be hurried. It is good practice to wait until everyone is still in the chapel before proceeding, keeping a final pause before speaking the preamble to the Committal and pressing the button. This measured approach is particularly important when the Committal alone is taking place following a church service. A Committal-only service may take no more than five or ten minutes. Arriving at the crematorium from the church, mourners can be thrown by just how quickly everything happens. Theoretically they know that they have come 'just for the Committal', but they can still be caught off guard.

Common Worship provides two alternative preambles to the act of Committal. The first is a recitation by the minister of verses from Psalm 103 beginning, 'The Lord is full of compassion and mercy'. The second preamble is a contemporary version of the words used in the Book of Common Prayer, itself a translation of the medieval text *Media vita*: 'In the midst of life we are in

death'. Ministers will select whichever text is better suited to the occasion, though the reference in the latter preamble to God being 'justly angered by our sins' means that many will prefer to recite verses from Psalm 103 that focus on the divine compassion.

Common Worship makes additional provision for the Committal to take place at the burial of the ashes rather than at the crematorium, but this option is rarely used. Most clergy prefer to use the now traditional prayer of Committal, perhaps raising their right hand in symbolic valediction, conscious that few people are likely to be present at the burial of the ashes:

> We have entrusted our *brother/sister* N to God's mercy,
> and we now commit *his/her* body to be cremated:
> earth to earth, ashes to ashes, dust to dust:
> in sure and certain hope of the resurrection to eternal life
> through our Lord Jesus Christ,
> who will transform our frail bodies
> that they may be conformed to his glorious body,
> who died, was buried, and rose again for us.
> To him be glory for ever. **Amen.** (p. 269)

Most crematoria have a button for the minister to press at this point. Contrary to what many assume, this does not automatically set things in motion but merely signals to the crematorium staff behind the scenes that the Committal is taking place. In some traditional crematoria the coffin, raised upon a catafalque, will begin to move away at this point to be received by those who operate the furnaces. In others a curtain may glide across to hide the coffin from view until the congregation has left the building, at which point the coffin is removed and the cremation proceeds. In a few crematoria nothing happens whatsoever – or indeed a family may stipulate that nothing should happen, the bereaved at the end of the service simply walking out of the chapel, leaving the coffin in full view on the catafalque. This is very unsatisfactory and, if at all possible, should be resisted. As it is, the disappearance of the coffin from view is not a true Committal, parallel to casting earth on to a coffin in a grave. To obscure the parting still further is

unhelpful. It may, in theory, protect a grieving family from the reality of death, but in the long run it is likely to be psychologically damaging and, at least from a Christian perspective, is theologically indefensible. A cremation, like a burial, must express the finality of death and not obscure it. The sense of loss and parting must not be glossed over. The movement of the coffin may indeed provoke an outpouring of grief and tears from assembled friends and relatives, but over time this will contribute to a speedier recovery. Furthermore the movement of the coffin away from the congregation at least mirrors the psychological reality of death. It is not we who have left the dead, it is they who have departed and left the land of the living.

Following the Committal the service needs to close with a selection of prayers and final music that brings the ceremony to a fitting conclusion. It is sensible to invite the congregation to sit following the Committal before launching into the closing prayers, so that they can adjust; otherwise what is spoken is likely to go over their heads. Following the blessing or the grace, when the minister leaves the chapel it is not unusual for a family to remain seated for a while, perhaps listening to some specially requested music as they compose themselves. In most crematoria either the funeral director or an attendant will escort the family to where any flowers that had accompanied the coffin are displayed. As at a church door, it is good if the minister greets each mourner personally, shaking them by the hand. For some people it may be their only contact with the clergy and the opportunity should not be squandered.

The burial of ashes

The conflicting customs of crematoria practice (as in the scattering of ashes) and church practice (the burial of ashes) are a direct consequence of the churches' initial lack of interest in the revival of the practice of cremation. The word 'ash', in fact a euphemism, is a generic term for cremated remains. In reality 'ashes' are pulverized bones. No uniform records have been maintained by British

crematoria that reveal the destiny of cremated remains, and there seems to be considerable variation in practice between urban and rural crematoria and between older and newer establishments. According to Davies, such statistics as are available suggest that on average 41 per cent of cremated remains are taken away and disposed of privately.[6]

With older crematoria the tradition established in the first half of the twentieth century was for ashes to be deposited at the crematorium where the cremation took place. In recent decades, and with a more mobile population, it is not unusual for relatives to request that the ashes of a loved one be sent and deposited at a different crematorium with which the family has links, perhaps because it was where a beloved parent was cremated some years previously. Their preference echoes the way a family might have an emotional link with a particular church or own a family burial plot.

In some places elaborate columbaria to house cremated remains have been constructed, most notably at Golders Green in north London. The term columbarium derives from the Latin *columba*, meaning dove, because the various niches and compartments for the ashes resembled the housing for doves and pigeons in a dovecot. Often modelled on ancient examples, columbaria are composed of galleries with niches in which urns or caskets containing the cremated remains of loved ones can be deposited, at least by those who can afford to do so.

In a village outside Devizes a farmer has received planning permission from Wiltshire County Council to create a 50-metre columbarium in one of his fields. It will contain seven circular chambers lined with niches for storing cinerary urns. When full it could contain the ashes of up to 2,400 people. In his application he says, 'This unique proposal will not harm the setting of the site and will produce an opportunity for addressing the desire to place a loved one's remains within an historic natural landscape.'[7] His aim is to create a twenty-first-century version of the prehistoric long barrow or burial chamber at nearby West Kennet. An

---

6 Davies, *Death, Ritual and Belief*, p. 29.
7 Report in *The Times*, London, Monday 26 August 2013, p. 18.

avowed atheist, he says, 'It will be a non-religious setting, which so many people want these days. The plan is to have three hundred niches and each family will have a niche. My family's ashes will be in one when we die . . . [The long barrow would be] set out in a precise orientation to relate to the position of the sunrise at the winter solstice.' Perhaps the farmer is drawing inspiration from nearby Stonehenge or from the prehistoric burial chamber at Newgrange in County Meath in Ireland at this point.

It is the responsibility of the family to decide when and where ashes should be disposed of. Usually they are held by the crematorium or funeral director until the family has decided what to do. Long barrows and exotic columbaria aside, most families ask for ashes to be buried or scattered in the grounds of crematoria, and this remains the most common pattern of disposal today. Ashes can also be buried in a pre-existing grave either in a churchyard or municipal cemetery, or interred in a specially designated garden of remembrance. Many churches have such dedicated gardens, particularly when the churchyard is closed to new interments. In the case of churchyards, the church provides a short form of service to accompany the burial of ashes, but in the case of crematoria their staff will supervise the disposal of ashes without ceremony or ritual. If no one claims the ashes a crematorium or funeral director will retain the cremated remains for a set period of time but then dispose of them in accordance with their company's policy.

Of course, there is no legal obligation for the next of kin to do any of these things. A person may collect the ashes of their relative, partner or friend and hang on to them for months or even years, storing them at home, much in the way they may be loath to dispose of the deceased's clothes or personal effects. They may find in their location under the stairs or in an urn on the sideboard a form of consolation, though most people would see it as unhealthy, an indication that they have yet to come to terms with the death. There is nothing to stop a mourner disposing of the ashes anywhere they wish, and many do: places they shared an affection for, a holiday destination, the golf course, the local woods where they walked or even the back garden. Cremation has opened up a wide variety of possibilities and rituals.

In Christian custom, cremated remains are buried not scattered, not least because they are bones. Although the Prayer Book antedated the possibility of cremation, it does make provision for the burial of a corpse at sea, and subsequent Canon Law has explicitly provided for the disposal of ashes at sea. This is usually done by placing the ashes directly into the sea rather than by lowering a casket of ashes. The broadcast scattering of ashes is seen as potentially unseemly or irreverent.

The emphasis in the disposal of ashes is always on reverence because the ground in which ashes are deposited is theologically equivalent to a grave: it is their resting place and to be respected. Liturgically it is why the prayer of Committal may be better used at the interment of ashes than at the crematorium. Their burial marks the true conclusion of the funeral rite. By the same token, chancellors of dioceses will seldom grant permission for the exhumation of bodies from churchyards in order that they might be reburied closer to a family. A grave, whether it contains a body or cremated remains, is to be honoured as the final resting place and left alone.

Common Worship provides an order for the burial of ashes that may include a brief service in church or take place entirely at the graveside or garden of remembrance, as the minister thinks fit. The ashes may be poured directly into the hole or interred in a small wooden casket (not plastic), much in the way a coffin would be buried. As an alternative to the prayer of Committal, the liturgy provides this prayer to accompany the deposition of ashes:

God our Father,
in loving care your hand has created us,
and as the potter fashions the clay
you have formed us in your image.
Through the Holy Spirit
you have breathed into us the gift of life.
In the sharing of love you have enriched our knowledge
of you and one another.
We claim your love today,
as we return these ashes to the ground

in sure and certain hope of the resurrection to eternal life. (p. 328)

In a traditional burial, nothing remains to be done after the funeral except to erect a cross or memorial stone at a later date, and then to tend the grave. A memorial plaque may similarly be erected where ashes are interred in a garden of remembrance or close by it. Whether or not a memorial plaque is subsequently erected, it is important that the minister record where and when the ashes were laid to rest.

12

Caring for the bereaved

Grief is a series of caves – dark, multiple and unfathomed. You do not explore them. You fall into them.

Richard Lischer[1]

One of the things that distinguishes humankind from the rest of the animal kingdom is tears. Animals create tears to wash the eyeball of debris, but as far as we know, human beings are the only ones who cry. We shed tears when we laugh and when we are sad. 'My tears have been my bread day and night, while all day long they say to me, "Where is now your God?"' (Ps. 42.3).

Among the collection of Roman artefacts in many museums are to be found lachrymatory bottles. These tiny glass bottles, often hexagonal in shape, are often found in excavations of ancient graves. They contained different things but most frequently tears. Mourners filled the glass bottles or cups with tears, and these were then placed in the grave as symbols of respect. Sometimes women were paid to cry into these vessels as they walked along in the mourners' procession to the grave, those crying the loudest and producing the most tears being generously rewarded. The greater the grief and the more tears that were shed, the more important and valued the deceased person was deemed to have been.

Tear bottles antedate the Roman Empire by hundreds of years. It is likely that they originated in the Ancient Near East, and there may be a reference to them in the psalms: '[Lord], You have

---

1 Richard Lischer (2013), *Stations of the Heart: Parting with a Son*, New York: Knopf, p. 220.

counted up my groaning; put my tears into your bottle; are they not written in your book?' (Ps. 56.8). Somewhat bizarrely, tear bottles made a comeback in nineteenth-century England. Victorians used to buy special bottles in which mourners could collect their tears. When the tears had evaporated, the period of mourning was deemed to have ended. It is claimed by some that the custom lies behind the English phrase 'to bottle it up', meaning to suppress or withhold your emotions.

Ancient and widespread mourning rituals such as these illustrate how universal the experience of grief is. The first question the angels ask Mary Magdalene as she stands sobbing beside the empty tomb on Easter morning is, 'Why are you weeping?' Indeed the risen Lord repeats the question, 'Woman, why are you weeping?' (John 20.13, 15). It sounds ridiculous to ask such a question, at least to us who know the end of the story. Obviously Mary was weeping because of the reality and finality of Jesus' death. But familiarity with the text of the Gospel can blunt our appreciation of just how candid the Christian view of death and resurrection is.

The Bible is consistently realistic about death and grief. One of the psalms speaks of grief in these words: 'When my prayer returned empty to my bosom, it was as though I grieved for my friend or brother. I behaved as one who mourns for his mother, bowed down and brought very low' (Ps. 35.14–15). The reason the message of Easter is so powerful is because it never pretends that death is not final or that it is trivial. What it goes on to proclaim is that in the resurrection of Jesus Christ, God initiates a new creation. Things are being made new and God invites us to share in the adventure. The book of Revelation looks forward to the day when God 'will wipe every tear from their eyes. Death will be no more; mourning and crying and pain will be no more' (Rev. 21.4). This conviction has the power to transform perspectives, with the result that we can look death in the face without fear. In the words of Paul, although we grieve, we should 'not grieve as others do who have no hope' (1 Thess. 4.13). Theologically this is what shapes the Church's ministry to the bereaved.

The journey of bereavement

In a fast-moving age it is easy to harbour unrealistic expectations of ourselves and others when it comes to adjusting to loss. It takes time to come to terms with death, even when its arrival has been anticipated after a protracted illness or in old age. Recovering an inner equilibrium and 'moving on' is not straightforward when your emotions are all over the place. Richard Lischer, following the tragic death of his son from a brain tumour, says, 'You are constantly righting yourself and daily, sometimes hourly, recovering from little plunges into unrequited longing and despair.'[2] As Rowan Williams points out, 'inhabiting grief is a matter of learning a landscape, recognizing an environment in which you are going to live for a long time, probably a lifetime.'[3]

In a preference for informality and in our distaste of ritual we have jettisoned the mourning customs that our Victorian forebears favoured, with their mourning bottles, black armbands and veils. But there was wisdom as well as ostentation in a system that publicized the pain of loss. The extended period of mourning dress the Victorians favoured had the merit of alerting strangers to a person's grief so that they made allowances for them. They recognized that grief could be visceral, reactions unpredictable and judgement uneven. These days you get a couple of days off for compassionate leave but are then expected to be back at work and to carry on as normal as if nothing has happened. There is gift in the resumption of routine, but there is also pressure.

Bereavement is less an interlude to be got through than a journey in which we discover emotions we didn't know we had. Nor is there anything short about it. Research confirms that on average the grieving process lasts two and half years, though at the time it can seem endless. It is why many bereavement counsellors are cautious about applying the language of 'closure' when it comes to grief. When you are bereaved it feels as if the darkness

---

2 Lischer, *Stations of the Heart*, p. 220.

3 Rowan Williams, *Inside Grief*, ed. Stephen Oliver, London: SPCK, 2013, p. ix.

will never lift, and of course for some it does not, or at least not entirely. There never is any light at the end of the tunnel. It is all very confusing and unsettling. If you catch yourself laughing and having fun you can easily feel overwhelmed by guilt, as if by smiling you have somehow betrayed the memory of the person you loved.

The explosion of emotions ignited by bereavement is well documented: grief, searing loss, anger, an endemic sadness that casts a grey pall over everything, anguish, rage (particularly in cases of suicide), relief (when the person has been ill for a long time and perhaps in considerable pain), loss of self-esteem, loneliness, despair, fear (How will I cope?), anxiety. Any and all of these things can surface on this roller-coaster ride. What is more, grief is like a Jack-in-the-box: it pops up when you least expect it.

One of the less documented aspects of bereavement is emotional and sexual disorientation – 'skin hunger' is how one widower described it. Depression is a frequent companion in bereavement, and depression suppresses libido. But sometimes this can jostle alongside an ache to be touched, to be held, to be caressed. The loss of physical intimacy, not necessarily sexual intimacy though that may be part of it, makes a bereaved person acutely vulnerable. I recall a young widow bravely confiding how sexually frustrated she felt following her husband's death. She felt so ashamed that in the midst of her grief she should be feeling like this. It is why maintaining appropriate pastoral boundaries is of the utmost importance in such conversations. A bereaved person may not know they are aching to be held and touched, and it is easy for a minister or counsellor to misread signals and inadvertently cross a line.

If the pastoral care of the bereaved is to be a reality and not just a slogan, we need to identify members of our congregations with time, sensitivity and good listening skills to be trained as bereavement visitors. Most dioceses offer training courses in bereavement visiting. Following up on funerals is too big and too important a task to be left to the clergy. Ideally it needs to be the responsibility of the whole community, but in the busyness of our lives it is easy for everyone's responsibility to become

no one's responsibility, with the result that the bereaved fall through the net and feel abandoned.

Some bereaved people may need help adjusting to new domestic realities. Death generates an avalanche of correspondence: personal, legal and financial. There may be letters of condolence that require acknowledgement. Not everyone has the capacity to handle such things efficiently. The obligation to register the death, organize the funeral, settle accounts and deal with the will are likely to keep the bereaved fully occupied for the first few weeks. But as the busyness subsides and the adrenaline stops pumping, the emerging emptiness can feel terrible. Three months after a funeral is often the low point in bereavement, and it is a key moment for the exercise of sensitive pastoral care. Maintaining contact with the bereaved is crucial.

Bereavement is a strange animal. Little things can set you off and open the floodgates: a photograph, spotting someone's handwriting on an old envelope or discovering their spare pair of spectacles stuffed at the back of a drawer. The journalist Melanie Reed revealed that it took her a whole year before she could summon up the courage to open up her dead mother's handbag.[4] Birthdays, wedding anniversaries, Mothering Sunday and Christmas can all be difficult times. The build-up to the first anniversary of death is likely to be huge. Pastorally it is a date that needs to be marked either by a card, flowers or a personal visit. A phone call from the minister who conducted the funeral can be a real consolation.

One of the things that often changes during bereavement is how the departed is viewed. When a death has been traumatic it may be some time before happier memories resurface alongside more painful episodes. Occasionally, suppressed information about a person may come to light after their death, which can be profoundly disturbing. When people die all sorts of secrets emerge, and a spouse or family can find themselves dealing with things that may have best remained hidden. Perspectives can alter and different things come into focus. In his *Confessions*, Augustine records his desolation following the death of his mother, Monica,

---

4 Melanie Reed, *The Times*, London, Saturday 19 October 2013.

but how his grief changed. Initially the intensity of his grief meant that he imprisoned his mother in aspic, making her into someone she was not. With the passage of time, however, he began to see her as she really was: a human being with faults and failings. The realization was releasing. Recovering a tapestry of memories and forging a more realistic view of the departed is part and parcel of the journey of bereavement. It is why it is such a privilege to accompany a person on this journey and help them rediscover their loved one as they genuinely were.

It is also why, to reiterate what has been said in the context of burials, there is wisdom in dissuading a bereaved family from commissioning a memorial to their loved one too quickly, whether erecting a headstone in a cemetery or placing a memorial tablet in a garden of remembrance where the cremated remains have been deposited. It is far better to let the tide of grief settle and subside before deciding on wording. The erection of a memorial can then become the occasion for cherishing memories and be a cairn on the journey from bereavement to remembering.

Holding a person's pain

The Bible is full of cautionary words about the tongue and the damage we can do by what we say and how we say it. A bereaved person is acutely sensitive to everything that is said to them, whether in jest or in sympathy. Words that sound spiritual and uplifting can, if ill-timed, do more harm than good. The book of Proverbs has a melancholy reflection about the way we can inadvertently make things worse by being too quick to cheer people up. 'Like one who takes off a garment on a cold day, like vinegar on a wound is one who sings songs to a heavy heart' (Prov. 25.20).

The rawness of people's grief can be disturbing. It can be difficult coping with one's own powerlessness in the face of an outpouring of emotion. Sister Frances Domenica, the founder of Helen House, the Children's Hospice in Oxford, has accompanied many parents as they sat helpless and distraught at the bedsides of their

terminally ill children. In her experience, rationalizing a death or using theological argument in such circumstances is likely to be counterproductive. In her view, 'raw grief . . . operates at a level much deeper than the intellect'.[5] Intellectualizing grief distances us from the bereaved and can unwittingly communicate that their pain isn't that important. Sitting and being present is the gift most bereaved people value. Such a ministry of presence can be particularly costly if the intensity of the person's grief puts us in touch with losses we have yet to come to terms with ourselves. In such situations it is tempting to distract people or attempt to change the subject. If we do, our words are likely to sound false and may easily descend into platitudes. We like to think that our words are always motivated by compassion but sometimes they may be driven more by fear, including the fear of self-scrutiny.

Paul characterizes an authentic Christian response with admirable succinctness: 'Rejoice with those who rejoice, weep with those who weep' (Rom. 12.15). His words encapsulate a mature spirituality, one rooted in demanding self-discipline and adept in personal skills that most of us have difficulty in learning. Anyone can share another's gladness; it is the ability to share another's sadness that reveals our true worth. In ministry among the bereaved we need to learn what questions to ask and when, but above all not to rush in with solutions and advice, neither of which may be wanted. We need to resist the temptation to fill up silences with easy reassurances or bright cheering comments.

In the book of Job the prophet's three friends meet together to console and comfort him in his loss. 'They sat with him on the ground for seven days and seven nights, and no one spoke a word to him, for they saw that his suffering was very great' (Job 2.13). Standing alongside someone in distress is not easy because we have a natural desire to make everything all right. But a lack of receptive silence will shut down a conversation, not open it up. If we are unwilling to stay for a few moments with someone's grief, raw and painful though it may be, it is likely that our meeting will

---

5 Sr Frances Dominica ASSP (2010), *Just My Reflection*, London: Darton, Longman & Todd, p. 35.

be experienced as a failure of companionship. The word companion literally means 'one with whom we share our bread', and there will be times when the only bread to be shared is the 'bread of adversity' (Isa. 30.20).

It is always a mistake to attempt to move a bereaved person on too quickly. I recall an undergraduate who lost her mother to cancer. The week after the funeral her father, in a desire to make a fresh start but without consulting his daughter, cleared out all his wife's clothes and took them to the local charity shop. It was way too soon for Jenny. Unknown to her father, she secretly bought all her mother's old clothes from the shop and stored them in her wardrobe back at college. She found the smell of them consoling because it reminded her of her mother. It was three years before she could finally part with them. When grief is smothered or short-circuited, all we succeed in doing is delaying the healing process.

Bereavement and memorial services

The month of November with its theme of remembrance is an ideal time to reach out to the bereaved. Many churches use this season as an opportunity to invite the friends and relatives of those who have had funerals taken by parish clergy and lay ministers in the past year or two to a special annual service of remembrance. Some parishes do this in partnership with local funeral directors, which is a wonderful way of honouring their pastoral ministry to their clients. Not only do such initiatives help build stronger working relationships with funeral directors but they also enable a church to keep in touch with those on the fringe who might otherwise hesitate to cross the threshold of our buildings.

In a culture where we are supposed to be relentlessly happy, our churches are acquiring a unique role as safe places where people can take off their masks without fear of ridicule and can express their grief. At memorial services, as at funerals, it is not uncommon to find people weeping, not necessarily for the person who has died but for someone else, perhaps a friend long since dead

but whose passing was never really faced up to. They may have bottled up their grief for years because it was too much to cope with at the time. Bereavement services can be held at any time of the year, but if held in November in the slow run-up to Christmas, whose arrival may be dreaded, they can be particularly poignant and a huge comfort to the bereaved.

Annual memorial services have their origin in medieval monastic custom. The Commemoration of all the Faithful Departed on 2 November following All Saints' Day, and traditionally known as All Souls' Day, began in France at the great Abbey of Cluny. From there the observance spread across Europe via its network of Cluniac houses, until by the thirteenth century it was universally observed throughout Western Europe. Although the observance did not survive the liturgical changes of the Reformation in England, largely because it had got muddled up with abuses associated with the 'unscriptural' medieval doctrine of Purgatory, the commemoration was reinstated in the calendar of the 1928 Prayer Book.

As the numerous inscriptions and prayers for peace and refreshment that cover the ancient catacombs in Rome reveal, prayer for the dead emerged in the general heart of the church as ordinary Christian men and women coped with death. These early prayers for 'rest' were not so much concerned with the repose of the soul after death – which was to become the case – as with the hope of Sabbath rest and festivity. Prayer for the dead in the early centuries was always positive and confident, born of a faith in the resurrection. It was a celebration of a Christian's possession of the kingdom. The *Martyrdom of Polycarp*, written around the year 155, provides evidence for the *natalicia* of martyrs, a celebration of their 'birthday' through the gateway of death, with the holding of an anniversary agape or commemorative Eucharist. Our modern commemorations of the faithful departed have their roots in these ancient observances.

In spite of a recovery of this primitive Christian perspective infused with Easter joy, some Anglicans remain ambivalent about praying for the dead, though united in their belief that all the faithful, both living and departed, are bound together in a communion of prayer. As with all prayer, the content of prayer for the departed

is love, not knowledge. I recall one elderly parishioner confiding to me that she continued to pray for her long-dead mother every night, closing her prayers by saying to God, 'Please give my love to mum.' The commemoration of the faithful departed enables us to remember before God with thanksgiving all those whom we have known personally, including those who gave us life, those who have sustained us by their love and loyalty, those who taught us the faith, all 'whom we love but see no longer'.

In high-church parishes this traditional annual commemoration of the faithful departed will most likely be expressed through the celebration of a Requiem Eucharist, usually on All Souls' Day itself. As we have noted, the commemoration of the dead in the context of the Eucharist and on their anniversary of death has a long and noble history. By the fourth century such commemorations were the norm. Augustine tells us that as his mother Monica lay dying she was not worried about where her body might be buried. To her that was incidental: 'Bury my body anywhere you like. Let no anxiety about that disturb you. I have only one request to make of you, that you remember me at the altar of the Lord, wherever you may be.'[6]

Some churches may prefer to hold a non-eucharistic service on, say, a Sunday afternoon, and there may be good pastoral reasons for doing so. Such a commemoration can be more easily tailored to the needs of the bereaved, many of whom may be on the fringes of the Church and will be unfamiliar with eucharistic worship. Whatever liturgical form is decided upon, the most important thing for the bereaved is likely to be seeing the minister who took the funeral again, reconnecting with him/her and hearing their loved one's name spoken aloud.

Bereavement services need to be well structured, quiet and not rushed, with opportunities for stillness and reflection without being unduly solemn. Hymns and music that offer both solace and lament should provide the mood music to enable the bereaved to enter the court of memory. If the church has a book of remembrance, it could be presented and displayed during the Bereavement

---

6 Augustine, *Confessions*, IX, x, 11.

service while suitable music is played. The names of the recently departed could be printed in the order of service. Better still their names should be read aloud, providing there are not too many of them, and candles lit in their memory, 'in sure and certain hope of the resurrection of the dead through our Lord Jesus Christ'. Such a formal commemoration creates a fitting focus for reflection and prayer. After the service, tea and refreshments can provide a relaxed setting in which bereaved and others can share memories and generally catch up.

From bereavement to remembering

The Christian minister is there for the whole journey, from death through bereavement and into remembering. In the course of it the bereaved are likely to find other loves forming 'a supporting web of new tissue and cartilage around [their] irreplaceable loss'[7] and thereby a degree of healing. The Christian will want to go further and in the light of Christ's resurrection recognize an eternal dimension to this journey. Augustine expresses this belief beautifully in a passage towards the end of his treatise, *The City of God*:

> In the heavenly city there will be freedom of will. There that precept from the psalms will find fulfilment: 'Be still and know that I am God.' That will truly be the greatest of Sabbaths; a Sabbath that has no evening, the Sabbath that the Lord approved at the beginning of creation. There we shall have leisure to be still, and we shall see that he is God. It will be an eighth day, as it were, which is to last for ever, a day consecrated by the resurrection of Christ, foreshadowing the eternal rest not only of the spirit but of the body also. There we shall be still and see; we shall see and we shall love; we shall love and we shall praise. Behold what will be, in the end without end![8]

---

7 Lischer, *Stations of the Heart*, p. 234.
8 Augustine, *The City of God*, XXII, 30.

13

Facing our mortality

It's only when we truly know and understand that we have a
limited time on earth . . . and that we have no way of knowing
when our time is up . . . that we will begin to live each day to
the full, as if it were the only one we had.

Elisabeth Kübler-Ross (1926–2004)

Richard Lischer, in his book *Stations of the Heart*, describes an
incident from his time as a newly ordained Lutheran priest when a
young woman confronted him after church one Sunday morning.
Standing in front of him she asked somewhat aggressively, 'What
does this church have to offer me?' Thrown by the directness of
her question and without paying attention to the look in her eyes,
like a fool he reeled off the most attractive features of their educational programme and church facilities. She said, 'Well, that's
nice, but I'm looking for someone to help me die. Do you think
your church is up to that? And what about you?' she asked. 'Is
that something you could do?'[1]

Is your church up to it? Is this something you could do? In
the Christian tradition, preparing for death and making 'a good
death' – whatever that might mean – is part of what it means to
follow Jesus Christ. This is never easy, and in a culture that glam-
orizes youth and beauty and regularly tidies death away, it can
be a huge challenge. It is certainly not a subject that the average
parish priest relishes exploring with parishioners. And yet in the
Litany of the Church we find these two ancient petitions:

---

1 Richard Lischer, 2013, *Stations of the Heart: Parting with a Son*, New
York: Knopf, p. 95.

From violence, murder and dying unprepared,
good Lord, deliver us.
In all times of sorrow;
in all times of joy;
in the hour of death,
and at the day of judgement,
good Lord, deliver us.[2]

Again, in the Visitation of the Sick, as set out both in the Book of Common Prayer and in *Common Worship*, one of the duties laid upon the priest is to encourage the sick to put their affairs in good order, to be reconciled with their neighbours and, if their conscience cannot be quietened, to make special confession of their sins before they die. In these ways a person might prepare themselves to meet their Maker. The old Prayer Book is uncompromising in its language:

Then shall the Minister examine whether [the sick person] repent him truly of his sins, and be in charity with all the world; exhorting him to forgive, from the bottom of his heart, all persons that have offended him; and if he have offended any other, to ask them forgiveness; and where he hath done injury or wrong to any man, that he make amends to the uttermost of his power. And if he have not before disposed of his goods, let him then be admonished to make his will, and to declare his debts, what he oweth, and what is owing unto him; for the better discharging of his conscience, and the quietness of his Executors. But men should often be put in remembrance to take order for the settling of their temporal estates whilst they are in health.

These words before rehearsed may be said before the Minister begin his Prayer, as he shall see cause. The Minister should not omit earnestly to move such sick persons as are of ability to be liberal to the poor.

---

2 'The Litany', *Common Worship*, p. 111.

Here shall the sick person be moved to make a special confession of his sins, if he feel his conscience troubled with any
weighty matter. After which confession, the Priest shall absolve
him (if he humbly and heartily desire it) after this sort.

When we are young we think we are immortal. But with the passing of the years we find illness and the shadow of death falling
across our path and we are no longer so sure. When a close member of our family dies or a friend or colleague at work is struck
down, we can be brought up short and suddenly confronted with
our mortality. We are reminded that the same fate awaits us. The
inevitability, if unpredictability, of death hovers in the background
and not always just in the background. 'I go to so many funerals
these days,' an elderly neighbour once said to me, 'and they're all
my friends.' The death of our parents is a huge thing to negotiate,
and the younger we are the more traumatic it is likely to be. Our
parents are always there for us. When they die we realize there is
no one between us and the grave. Suddenly we find ourselves next
in the queue.

We all find ways of forgetting about death and use benign
expressions that attempt to empty it of finality or threat. We talk
about 'passing away' or 'crossing over to the other side'. As T. S.
Eliot lamented, 'Human kind cannot bear very much reality.'[3] Yet
it should be the Christian instinct to face the prospect of death
square on. Thinking about death, including our own, does not
have to be a grisly, morbid affair. On the contrary, it is good for
us. It liberates us to live now in the present moment and not fritter
away our days in the pursuit of trivia. It forces us to reflect on our
priorities, our relationships and the way we are living.

Malcolm Muggeridge once likened death to approaching harbour
at the end of a long sea voyage.[4] At the outset of the voyage, he said,
we tend to be interested only in whether or not we have a decent

---

3 T. S. Eliot, 'Burnt Norton, I', *Four Quartets*, London: Faber & Faber,
1935.

4 Quoted in Richard Harries (2002), *God Outside the Box*, London:
SPCK, p. 122.

cabin complete with a good porthole from which to admire the view. As the voyage progresses we are drawn to our fellow passengers, particularly those we find interesting and attractive. We can become obsessed with our status and whether we will be invited to sit at the Captain's table. However, as the harbour comes into view all of this falls away. Personal comfort, ambition, status, success, whether the world is taking note of us, seem of little consequence. The destination is much more important. Its proximity precipitates some unpalatable questions:

- Am I making the best of my life?
- What do I really want?
- Am I living in a way that accords with my conscience?
- Are there things I need to let go of?
- Are there relationships I need to sort out?

Luther is alleged to have remarked that if he knew he was going to die tomorrow, he would plant a tree today. So much for Luther. If we knew we were going to die tomorrow, what would we do today? It's worth thinking about. It's also worth thinking about what epitaph we would like inscribed on our gravestone – not that we will have any say in the matter. Questions such as these invite us to reflect on how other people experience us. How should we live now to be worthy of the epitaph we desire? Faced with our mortality and confronted with challenges such as these, we can find ourselves growing in maturity almost overnight. But we may need help. It is a lonely path to tread.

A custom that began in some Jewish communities during the Middle Ages was to write what today is sometimes called 'an ethical will'. Life expectancy was short and childbirth was dangerous. As a result it became the custom of Jewish women to create boxes filled with objects of sentimental value that they wanted to pass on to their children, knowing that they might never live to see them grow up. With these objects they used to write letters in which they described the lessons they had learnt in life and what values they wanted their children and grandchildren to embody. Sometimes the letters were expressions of thanks or advice about

what to do when money is short or when a marriage is in difficulty. Writing letters to family and loved ones to be read after our
death is an honourable tradition, worthy of greater use.

Like the Jew, the Christian faces death realistically but also in
the faith that issues from the resurrection of Christ – that death
is a gateway, a new beginning, a fulfilment of human life, not its
eclipse. We are pilgrims moving towards the harbour of fulfilment
in God. It is healthy to look forward to that final destination. It
must consist in an experience of love because love is the highest of
all human experiences: to love totally and to be loved completely.
It is in union with all that is most lovable that we become fully
ourselves.

In 1999 the late Cardinal Hume astounded the media when he
announced that he had advanced cancer and spoke of his immi-
nent death, saying:

> I have received two wonderful graces. First, I have been given
> time to prepare for a new future. Secondly, I find myself unchar-
> acteristically calm and at peace. I intend to carry on working
> as much and as long as I can. I have no intention of being an
> invalid until I have to submit to the illness. But nevertheless I
> shall be a bit limited in what I can do. Above all no fuss. The
> future is in God's hands.

Like Basil Hume, it is possible to choose to live our lives in
relationship with the God who has revealed himself to us in Jesus
Christ. We can be confident of his promise: 'I came that they may
have life, and have it abundantly' (John 10.10). His words cultivate within me a sense of travelling home to God. As a result I
face my mortality in the conviction that death is not extinction
but the gateway to the fulfilment of my life. God enriches and
transforms human existence into life and life into a pilgrimage.
Any fears that haunt me tend to be more about the process of
dying than the event itself. Dying is not the issue. It is living until
I die and living it well and to the glory of God.

Through prayer I endeavour to inhabit my life fully. I endeavour to entrust the past to God's mercy, the present to his grace

and the future to his providence. Perhaps we all need to make John Henry Newman's prayer, so often used at the close of funerals, our own and to pray it daily:

> Support us, O Lord,
> all the day long of this troublous life,
> until the shadows lengthen and the evening comes,
> the busy world is hushed,
> the fever of life is over
> and our work is done.
> Then, Lord, in your mercy, grant us a safe lodging,
> a holy rest, and peace at the last;
> through Christ our Lord. Amen.[5]

---

5 A prayer originally written by John Henry Newman (1801–90) and now used frequently at funeral services, including that authorized by *Common Worship* (pp. 272, 362).

Appendix A

Canon Law and funerals

Canon B 38.2

It shall be the duty of every minister to bury, according to the rites of the Church of England, the corpse or ashes of any person deceased within his cure or of any parishioners or persons whose names are entered on the church electoral roll of his parish whether deceased within his cure or elsewhere that is brought to a church or burial ground or cemetery under his control in which the burial or interment of such corpse or ashes may lawfully be effected, due notice being given; except the person deceased have died unbaptized, or being of sound mind have laid violent hands upon himself, or have been declared excommunicate for some grievous and notorious crime and no man to testify to his repentance; in which case and in any other case at the request of the relative, friend, or legal representative having charge of or being responsible for the burial he shall use at the burial such service as may be prescribed or approved by the Ordinary, being a service neither contrary to, nor indicative of any departure from, the doctrine of the Church of England in any essential matter: Provided that, if a form of service available for the burial of suicides is approved by the General Synod under Canon B2, that service shall be used where applicable instead of the aforesaid service prescribed or approved by the Ordinary, unless the person having charge or being responsible for the burial otherwise requests.

In highlighting Canon B38 readers should be alert to the danger of supposing that this is the only law on burial as far as the Church of England is concerned. In fact there have been numerous Acts of Parliament that regulate this, as well as Synodical regulation. An excellent overview of funerals in relation to the Canon Law of the Church of England is provided by Rupert D. H. Bursell (1996), *Liturgy, Order and the Law*, Oxford: Clarendon, pp. 199–215. Readers should also take note of the current (8th) edition of *Legal Opinions Concerning the Church of England*.

Appendix B

Sample funeral record and invoice

Funeral details

Service date [   ]   Time [   ]

Name of deceased [   ]

Date of death [   ]   Aged [   ]

Address [   ]

Next of kin [   ]

Relationship [   ]

Address [   ]

Tel. [   ]

Email [   ]

Funeral director [   ]

Burial or cremation (state location)

[   ]

Time of funeral [   ]

Arrangements made by church

Minister	

Tick when paid

Organist		

Verger/s		

Service information

Hymns	
Bible reading/s	
Eulogy by?	
Poems etc.?	
CD use? Please list song and name of person nominated to operate player	
Any other info.?	

This should be emailed to all staff

Church Name and address here	Church Logo goes here

INVOICE

Date of funeral service

Name of deceased

Funeral director

Service (in church, cemetery or crematorium)	
Burial in churchyard following on from service in church	
Burial certificate, if required	
Verger	
Organist	
Total	

This payment may be made by BACS (give details) or cheque payable to (insert who payable) and sent to the above address.

Payment must be received no later than (date of service).

Appendix C

Funeral hymns

Psalms

The twenty-third psalm is the best known and best loved of all the psalms and it is the standard choice at funerals. However, other psalms are equally appropriate and may be better suited to the occasion:

    1, 15, 46, 90, 121, 130, 139 vv. 1–18

If the congregation is small it may be advisable to say the psalm together. If the congregation is large a metrical version of a psalm might work well.

'All people that on earth do dwell' by William Kethe
    Tune: Old hundredth (Psalm 100)
'O God our help in ages past' by Isaac Watts
    Tune: St Anne (Psalm 46)
'The King of love my shepherd is' by H. W. Baker
    Tune: Dominus regit me or St Columba (Psalm 23)
'The Lord's my shepherd' from the Scottish Psalter
    Tune: Crimond or Brother James' Air (Psalm 23)
'Through all the changing scenes of life' by Tate and Brady
    Tune: Wiltshire (Psalm 34)

Hymns

'Abide with me' by H. F. Lyte
    Tune: Eventide

'All things bright and beautiful' by Cecil Frances Alexander
Tune: Royal Oak or All things bright and beautiful
'Amazing Grace' by John Newton
Tune: Amazing Grace
'Be thou my vision' traditional Irish, translated by Mary Byrne
Tune: Slane
'Blest are the pure in heart' by John Keble
Tune: Franconia
'Dear Lord and Father of mankind' by John Greenleaf Whittier
Tune: Repton
'Eternal Father strong to save' by William Whiting
Tune: Melita
'For all the saints who from their labours rest' by W. Walsham
How
Tune: Sine nomine
'Great is thy faithfulness' by Thomas Chisholm
Tune: Faithfulness
'Guide me, O thou great Redeemer' by William Williams
Tune: Cwm Rhondda
'He who would valiant be' by John Bunyan
Tune: Monks Gate
'I am the Bread of life' by Suzanne Toolan
Tune: I am the bread of life
'I heard the voice of Jesus say' by Horatius Bonar
Tune: Kingsfold
'Immortal, invisible, God only wise' by W. Chalmers Smith
Tune: St Denio
'Jerusalem the golden' by Bernard of Cluny
Tune: Ewing
'Just as I am, without one plea' by Charlotte Elliott
Tune: Saffron Walden
'Lead us, heavenly Father, lead us' by James Edmeston
Tune: Mannheim
'Lord for the years' by Timothy Dudley-Smith
Tune: Lord for the years
'Lord of all hopefulness' by Jan Struther
Tune: Slane

'Love Divine, all loves excelling' by Charles Wesley
Tune: Blaenwern or Love Divine
'Make me a channel of your peace' by Sebastian Temple
Tune: St Francis
'Morning has broken' by Eleanor Farjeon
Tune: Bunessan
'Now thank we all our God' by Martin Rinkart
Tune: Nun danket
'O Jesus I have promised' by John Ernest Bode
Tune: Wolvercote or Hatherop Castle
'O Lord my God, when I in awesome wonder' by Stuart J. Hine
Tune: How great thou art
'O Love that wilt not let me go' by G. Matheson
Tune: St Margaret
'Praise my soul, the King of Heaven' by H. F. Lyte
Tune: Praise my soul
'Praise to the Holiest in the height' by John Henry Newman
Tune: Gerontius or Chorus Angelorum
'Rock of ages' by A. M. Toplady
Tune: Petra
'The day thou gavest, Lord, is ended' by J. Ellerton
Tune: St Clement
'The old rugged cross' by George Bernard
Tune: The old rugged cross
'The strife is o'er, the battle done' by Francis Pott
Tune: Victory
'Thine be the glory' by Edmond Budry, translated by Richard Hoyle
Tune: Maccabeus
'To God be the glory' by Frances J. van Alstyne
Tune: To God be the glory
'When all thy mercies, O my God' by Joseph Addison
Tune: Contemplation
'When I survey the wondrous cross' by Isaac Watts
Tune: Rockingham

Appendix D

Glossary

Absolution A formal declaration of the forgiveness of sins. The declaration of God's forgiveness is pronounced by the priest acting upon the commission of Christ to 'bind' and 'loose' (Matt. 16.19; 18.18; John 20.23). An absolution is usually accompanied by the priest making the sign of the cross over the person or congregation.

Act of Contrition A prayer of sorrow and penitence said by a person when making a private confession to a priest, often when they are gravely ill or near death.

Agnus dei A devotional anthem introduced in the seventh century to accompany the breaking of the consecrated bread during the Eucharist. The phrase comes from the opening Latin words meaning 'Lamb of God'. As early as the eleventh century a variant appeared at requiem masses for the dead, when the phrase 'grant them eternal rest' was substituted.

Ash A generic term for cremated remains. In reality 'ashes' are pulverized bones.

Back filling The custom of friends and relatives staying behind after the funeral to fill in the grave themselves.

Bearers Those who carry or 'bear' the coffin on their shoulders, also known as 'pall-bearers'.

Bidding Prayer An invitation to prayer and worship, often specially composed for an important occasion such as a memorial service. Biddings are addressed to the congregation, inviting them to pray, and may punctuate prayers of intercession.

Bier Some ancient parish churches still boast their own parish bier – the pallet or trolley on which a coffin is transported to and from the church and then to the graveside.

Bier lights Tall candlesticks that stand beside a coffin during a funeral service. There may be two, four or six, used in pairs, according to local custom. The candles used were typically of unbleached wax but this custom has gone somewhat out of fashion.

Canon The Greek word *kanon* means a rule or measuring rod, and came to be applied to the rules for the ordering of worship, including funeral services – hence the 'Canons of the Church of England'.

Catafalque A raised bier or plinth on which is set the coffin during a funeral, particularly at a crematorium. The term originates from the Italian *catafalco*, meaning scaffolding.

Certificate of Disposal The authorization by a registrar (in England and Wales) or procurator fiscal (in Scotland) giving permission for burial or cremation to proceed.

Chapel of rest A designated room in the premises of a funeral director in which the body of the deceased can be viewed by members of the family prior to the funeral.

Columbarium A structure composed of galleries with niches to house urns or caskets containing cremated remains. The term derives from the Latin *columba*, meaning dove, because the various niches and compartments for the ashes resembled the housing for doves and pigeons in a dovecot.

Commendation A form of prayer used at the time of death, commending the person into the loving arms of God.

Commendation and Farewell The solemn climax of the offering of prayer during a funeral service when the deceased is formally commended to the keeping of God and the family bids farewell, prior to the committal of the body for burial or cremation.

Committal The committal of a body to be buried or cremated during which authorized words are spoken by the officiating minister.

Confession From the Latin *confessio*, meaning 'I confess'. The term refers to an act of penitence and may be used in two principal ways: to denote either a general confession said by all during an act of worship; or a confession of sins to a priest in private, for which the Church makes special liturgical provision.

Consecrated ground From the Latin *consecratio*, referring to the act of setting apart land for Christian burial by the bishop.

Death Certificate Properly termed a 'Medical Certificate of Cause of Death' and issued by the doctor if he or she is satisfied with the cause of death.

Dismissal From the Latin *dismissus*, meaning 'sent away'. The title designates the end of a gathering for worship, including a funeral, when the congregation is 'dismissed', sent out in the peace of Christ.

Easter candle The great Easter (Paschal) candle burns throughout Eastertide until and including the Day of Pentecost. It is placed on a large candlestick in a prominent place in church. Outside Eastertide it is usually placed near the font to underline the link between baptism and dying and rising with Christ. At funerals it is often placed next to the coffin to symbolize the hope of resurrection.

Eulogy From the Greek, literally meaning 'good words'. The word may be used instead of 'tribute', referring to a personal address offered by a relative or friend in memory of the deceased at a funeral or memorial service.

Green funerals Environmentally friendly burials where bodies are interred in natural or woodland sites in biodegradable coffins usually made of wicker or cardboard. No gravestones or memorials are erected.

Nunc dimittis The Song of Simeon when he picked up the child Jesus in the temple and recognized him to be the Messiah (Luke 2.29–32). It begins, 'Now you dismiss your servant in peace'. Its title comes from its opening words in Latin. The canticle is said or sung regularly at Evensong and Compline but is often also recited by a minister when leading a coffin out of church at the end of a funeral.

Occasional offices The title used for a range of pastoral services, including baptisms, marriages, funerals and ministry to the sick.

Pall From the Latin *pallium*, meaning 'cloak', and thus used of any cloth that envelops or covers an object. In the context of funerals the term is used of the large, heavy hanging sometimes used to cover a coffin.

Paschal candle See Easter candle.

Post-mortem An official examination of the body authorized by the registrar to ascertain the cause of death. Also known as an autopsy.

Propers Those parts of the liturgy that are variable ('appropriate') and change with a feast day or season.

Reader A person who has received theological training and is licensed by the bishop to assist the clergy in the leading of public worship and in preaching. Readers – formerly known as Lay Readers – are invested with a blue preaching scarf as a sign of their office. They may also undergo supplementary training and be authorized to conduct funerals with the knowledge and agreement of both incumbent and family.

Requiem From the Latin *requiem*, meaning 'rest', and more properly termed Requiem Mass. It denotes a Eucharist celebrated in memory of a dead person either at their funeral or soon after, or on the annual commemoration of the faithful departed on 2 November (All Souls' Day). In popular usage the word refers to a number of musical settings that may be performed independently of liturgical commemoration. The term comes from the Latin introit of the service, 'Grant unto them eternal rest'.

Responsorial psalm A psalm sung responsively by cantor or choir and congregation.

Rigor mortis Chemical changes in the muscles that cause a dead body to stiffen and become difficult to move or manipulate.

Robes A general term for special clothes worn during worship by clergy and others.

Rubrics From the Latin *ruber*, meaning 'red': the ceremonial directives for liturgy, customarily printed in medieval prayer books using red ink to distinguish them from the text of prayers. *Common Worship* has returned to this convention, though not all modern prayer books do. Regardless of colour, the term 'rubric' is still used to mean ceremonial directions.

Sentences In Anglican custom, funerals usually begin with the minister leading the coffin into church, reciting short sentences of Scripture that declare both the finality of death and belief in the resurrection.

Sexton The person with oversight of a churchyard.

Sprinkling Technically 'asperges', from the Latin *aspergere*, meaning 'to sprinkle'. The word comes from the Latin translation of the verse, 'You will sprinkle me with hyssop and I shall be clean; you will wash me and I shall be whiter than snow' (Ps. 51.7), customarily recited by the priest when sprinkling a congregation with water in remembrance of their baptism. Sprinkling may also occur in the context of a funeral service, either when the coffin is greeted at the church door by the priest or during the Commendation and Farewell. It may also occur at the graveside if the grave is not in consecrated ground and has not been blessed.

Testimony A personal statement of faith.

Tribute A personal address or eulogy, often given by a relative or colleague at a funeral or memorial service in memory of the deceased.

Verger (Virger) From the Latin *virga*, meaning 'rod'. The name given to someone who looks after the interior of a church and who in processions customarily carries a 'virge', a wand of office. In some parishes a verger may lead the minister and coffin up the aisle at the beginning of the funeral.

Viewing A colloquial term for viewing a body at a chapel of rest.

Year's mind The custom of remembering publicly a deceased person in prayer on the anniversary of their death. This may be done in the context of the regular intercessions on a Sunday or at a special Eucharist (Requiem), particularly on the first anniversary of death. Names may be inscribed in a book of remembrance and kept in a prominent place in a church.

Appendix E

Readings and reflections for funerals and memorial services

This selection of readings is not exhaustive, but seeks to be a resource to those ministering among the bereaved or who find themselves trying to put together an order of service for a funeral or memorial service. They are not here to replace readings from Scripture but to supplement them.

On the death of his son

I loved the boy with the utmost love of which my soul is capable, and he is taken from me – yet in the agony of my spirit in surrendering such a treasure I feel a thousand times richer than if I had never possessed it.

William Wordsworth
written in 1812 on the death of his six-year-old son, Thomas

Death

Death is not the extinguishing of the light
but the blowing out of the candle
because the dawn has come.

Rabindranath Tagore

How do I love thee? Let me count the ways

How do I love thee? Let me count the ways.
I love thee to the depth and breadth and height

My soul can reach, when feeling out of sight
For the ends of being and ideal grace.
I love thee to the level of every day's
Most quiet need, by sun and candlelight.
I love thee freely, as men strive for right;
I love thee purely, as they turn from praise.
I love thee with the passion put to use
In my old griefs, and with my childhood's faith.
I love thee with a love I seemed to lose
With my lost saints – I love thee with the breath,
Smiles, tears, of all my life! – and, if God choose,
I shall but love thee better after death.

Elizabeth Barrett Browning
Sonnets from the Portuguese

You can shed tears that she is gone

You can shed tears that she is gone,
or you can smile because she has lived.
You can close your eyes and pray that she'll come back,
or you can open your eyes and see all that she's left.
Your heart can be empty because you can't see her,
or you can be full of the love you shared.
You can turn your back on tomorrow and live yesterday,
or you can be happy for tomorrow because of yesterday.
You can remember her and only that she's gone,
or you can cherish her memory and let it live on.
You can cry and close your mind, be empty and turn your back,
or you can do what she'd want:
smile, open your eyes, love and go on.

Anonymous
Read at the Funeral of Queen Elizabeth, the Queen Mother

The Loom of Time

Man's life is laid in the loom of time
    To a pattern he does not see,
While the weavers work and the shuttles fly
    Till the dawn of eternity.

Some shuttles are filled with silver threads
    And some with threads of gold,
While often but the darker hues
    Are all that they may hold.

But the weaver watches with skilful eye
    Each shuttle fly to and fro,
And sees the pattern so deftly wrought
    As the loom moves sure and slow.

God surely planned the pattern:
    Each thread, the dark and fair,
Is chosen by his master skill
    And placed in the web with care.

He only knows its beauty,
    And guides the shuttles which hold
The threads so unattractive,
    As well as the threads of gold.

Not till the loom is silent,
    And the shuttles cease to fly,
Shall God reveal the pattern
    And explain the reason why

The dark threads were as needful
    In the weaver's skilful hand
As the threads of gold and silver
    For the pattern which he planned.

Anonymous

Remember me

Remember me when I am gone away,
Gone far away into the silent land;
When you can no more hold me by the hand,
Nor I half turn to go yet turning stay.
Remember me when no more day by day
You tell me of our future that you planned:
Only remember me; you understand
It will be late to counsel then or pray.
Yet if you should forget me for a while
And afterwards remember, do not grieve:
For if the darkness and corruption leave
A vestige of the thoughts that once I had,
Better by far you should forget and smile
Than that you should remember and be sad.

Christina Rossetti

How did he live?

Not, how did he die, but how did he live?
Not, what did he gain, but what did he give?
These are the units to measure the worth
Of a man as a man, regardless of birth.
Not what was his church, nor what was his creed?
But had he befriended those really in need?
Was he ever ready, with word of good cheer,
To bring back a smile, to banish a tear?
Not what did the sketch in the newspaper say,
But how many were sorry when he passed away?

Anonymous

The Pilgrim's Progress

After this it was noised abroad, that Mr Valiant-for-truth was taken with a summons by the same post as the other; and had this for a token that the summons was true, 'That his pitcher was broken at the fountain.' When he understood it, he called for his friends, and told them of it. Then, said he, 'I am going to my Father's; and though with great difficulty I am got hither, yet now I do not repent me of all the trouble I have been at to arrive where I am. My sword I give to him that shall succeed me in my pilgrimage, and my courage and skill to him that can get it. My marks and scars I carry with me, to be a witness for me, that I have fought his battles who now will be my rewarder.' When the day that he must go hence was come, many accompanied him to the river side, into which as he went he said, 'Death, where is thy sting?' And as he went down deeper, he said, 'Grave, where is thy victory?' So he passed over, and all the trumpets sounded for him on the other side.

John Bunyan

What is dying?

A ship sails and I stand watching till she fades on the horizon, and someone at my side says, 'She is gone'. Gone where? Gone from my sight, that is all; she is just as large as when I saw her. The diminished size and total loss of sight is in me, not in her, and just at the moment when someone at my side says, 'She is gone', there are others who are watching her coming, and other voices take up a glad shout, 'Here she comes!' . . . and that is dying.

Bishop Charles Brent

Death be not proud

Death be not proud, though some have called thee
    Mighty and dreadful, for, thou art not so,
    For, those, whom thou think'st, thou dost overthrow,
Die not, poor Death, nor yet canst thou kill me;

From rest and sleep, which but thy pictures be,
    Much pleasure, then from thee, much more must flow;
    And soonest our best men with thee do go,
Rest of their bones, and soul's delivery.
Thou art slave to fate, chance, kings, and desperate men,
    And dost with poison, war, and sickness dwell,
    And poppy, or charms can make us sleep as well,
And better than thy stroke. Why swell'st thou then?
    One short sleep past, we wake eternally,
    And death shall be no more: Death thou shalt die.

John Donne

Only an horizon

We seem to give them back, to thee, O God,
who gavest them to us.
Yet as thou did'st not lose them when thou gavest them to us,
so we do not lose them by their return.
Not as the world giveth, givest thou, O Lover of souls.
What thou givest, thou takest not away,
for what is thine is ours also if we are thine.
And life is eternal and love is immortal,
and death is only an horizon,
and an horizon is nothing save the limit of our sight.
Lift us up, strong Son of God,
that we may see further;
draw us closer to thyself,
that we may know ourselves to be nearer to our loved ones
who are with thee.
And while thou dost prepare a place for us,
prepare us also for that happy place,
that where thou art there we may be also for evermore. Amen.

William Penn
from *Fruits of Solitude*

After a suicide

Why?
She could have rung me.
Perhaps I should have rung her?
Do you think it would have made any difference – if I'd rung
   her I mean?
That night.
I was out, but she could have left a message,
and I would have phoned her back.

I knew she was depressed, but I didn't know it was that bad.
Why didn't she say?
She was such a private person.
At times, you know, she just clammed up.
She could be infuriating like that.
How could she do this?
God, I'm so angry.
I mean, all she had to do was pick up the phone.
I would have come.
I can't stop thinking about it all and wondering.
I can't get her face out of my mind.
My mind goes round and round in circles.
Do you think she died in pain? Did the doctor say anything?
God I hope not.
Was there a note? Do you know what it said?
Unbelievable. What a mess.
I hope she knew I cared.
I really loved her, you know.
Looking back, I wish I had told her that now.
I mean I'm sure she knew, but I wish I had just told her, that's all.
Sometimes it wasn't easy to talk.
She had that far away look in her eyes,
as if she were imprisoned behind a glass screen and couldn't get out.
Remote.
If only I could understand.

Anonymous

Take him, earth, for cherishing

Take him, earth, for cherishing,
To thy tender breast receive him.
Body of a man I bring thee,
Noble even in its ruin.

Once was this a spirit's dwelling,
By the breath of God created.
High the heart that here was beating,
Christ the prince of all its living.

Guard him well, the dead I give thee,
Not unmindful of his creature
Shall he ask it: He who made it
Symbol of his mystery.

Come the hour God hath appointed
To fulfil the hope of men,
Then must thou, in very fashion,
What I give, return again.

Not though ancient time decaying
Wear away these bones to sand,
Ashes that a man might measure
In the hollow of his hand:

Not though wandering winds and idle,
Drifting through the empty sky,
Scatter dust was nerve and sinew,
Is it given man to die.

Once again the shining road
Leads to ample paradise;
Open are the woods again
That the serpent lost for men.

Take, O take him, mighty Leader,
Take again thy servant's soul,
To the house from which he wandered
Exiled, erring, long ago.

But for us, heap earth about him,
Earth with leaves and violets strewn,
Grave his name, and pour the fragrant
Balm upon the icy stone.

By the breath of God created
Christ the prince of all its living
Take, O take him,
Take him, earth, for cherishing.

Prudentius

Postcards to a dead friend

Since you died,
I've wondered where you are,
questioned hell and threatened heaven.
Is there a place for those who say they don't believe?
When you were sixteen,
you said that you'd believe when you were older,
maybe forty.
You barely got half way.

Since you died,
I think about my growing years differently.
How dare you
take my memories and paint them
with the bitter vinegar of your sad sorrows?
I had enough already.

Since you died,
I see your parents differently.
Solitary walks do not mean peaceful rambles,
and framed photographs are not artistic expression.
They looked like they'd been winded for months.

Since you died,
I've thought about you
more than I had in years.

Called you a dickhead most often,
and lurched at what caused
your final purging.

Since you died,
you will grow no older now –
the twenty-four year old Peter Pan
of your mother's mind.
Her lost boy,
caught in the never-never land
between the grave and the sky.

Pádraig Ó Tuama
From *Readings from the Book of Exile*

Never weather-beaten sail

Never weather-beaten sail more willing bent to shore,
  Never tired pilgrim's limbs affected slumber more,
Than my weary spright now longs to fly out of my troubled
breast.
  O! come quickly, sweetest Lord, and take my soul to rest.

Ever blooming are the joys of heaven's high paradise.
  Cold age deafs not there our ears, nor vapour dims our
   eyes;
Glory there the sun outshines, whose beams the blessed only see.
  O! come quickly, glorious Lord, and raise my spright to
   thee.

Thomas Campion

The final awakening

Death, the last sleep?
No, the final awakening.

Sir Walter Scott

Crossing the bar

Sunset and evening star,
    And one clear call for me!
And may there be no moaning of the bar,
    When I put out to sea,

But such a tide as moving seems asleep,
    Too full for sound and foam,
When that which drew from out the boundless deep
    Turns again home.

Twilight and evening bell,
    And after that the dark!
And may there be no sadness of farewell,
    When I embark;

For though from out our bourne of Time and Place
    The flood may bear me far,
I hope to see my Pilot face to face
    When I have crost the bar.

                                Alfred, Lord Tennyson

Appendix F

Select bibliography

Ainsworth-Smith, Ian and Speck, Peter (1982), *Letting Go: Caring for the Dying and Bereaved*, London: SPCK.

Atwell, Robert (2005), *Remember: 100 Readings in Death and Bereavement*, Norwich: Canterbury Press.

Bentley, James, Best, Andrew and Hunt, Jackie (eds) (1994), *Funerals: a Guide to Prayers, Hymns and Readings*, London: Hodder & Stoughton.

Brind, Jan and Wilkinson, Tessa (2008), *Funeral, Memorial and Thanksgiving Services*, Norwich: Canterbury Press.

Brooks, Jeremy (2013), *Heaven's Morning Breaks*, Stowmarket: Kevin Mayhew.

Davies, Douglas J. (2002), *Death, Ritual and Belief: The Rhetoric of Funerary Rites*, London and New York: Continuum.

Graham, Jim (1984), *Dying to Live: The Christian Teaching on Life after Death*, Basingstoke: Marshall, Morgan & Scott.

Hinton, John (1967), *Dying*, London and New York: Penguin.

Horton, R. Anne, *Using Common Worship: Funerals*, London: CHP, 2000.

Lewis, C. S. (1961), *A Grief Observed*, London and Boston: Faber & Faber.

Rowell, Geoffrey (1977), *The Liturgy of Christian Burial*, London: Alcuin Club/SPCK.

Sheppy, Paul (2003), *In Sure and Certain Hope: Liturgies, Prayers and Readings for Funerals and Memorial Services*, Norwich: Canterbury Press.

Walter, Tony (1990), *Funerals and How to Improve Them*, London: Hodder & Stoughton.

Acknowledgements

Every effort has been made to trace copyright ownership of material included in this book. The author and publishers apologize to those who have not been traced at the time of going to press or whose rights have inadvertently not been acknowledged. They would be grateful to be informed of any omissions or inaccuracies in this respect.

Material from *Common Worship: Pastoral Services*, including the Psalter, is copyright © The Archbishops' Council, 2000, and is used with permission. Apart from the psalms, all other biblical quotations are taken from the *New Revised Standard Version*, Anglicized Edition, © 1989, 1995, The Division of Christian Education of the National Council of Churches in the USA.

The author and publisher are grateful to the University of Chester (Department of Media) for permission to share the – as yet – unpublished findings from its funeral project in and around Warrington conducted by J. Brookman, B. Davies, I. Delinger, L. Gittins, S. Kimmance, J. Proudfoot, C. Watkins and S. Wright, 'Church of England: Deanery of Great Budworth Funeral Project' (2012), Chester: University of Chester.

The author and publisher are grateful to the following copyright holders for permission to reproduce material under copyright:

Alcuin Club/SPCK, for a quotation from Geoffrey Rowell (1977), *The Liturgy of Christian Burial*.

SPCK, for a quotation from Stephen Oliver (ed.) (2013), *Inside Grief*.

Bible Reading Fellowship, for a quotation from Jeremy Fletcher (2013), *Rules for Reverends*.

Continuum, for a quotation from Douglas J. Davies (2002), *Death, Ritual and Belief*.

ACKNOWLEDGMENTS

David Higham Associates, for an extract from Dylan Thomas's poem, 'Do Not Go Gentle Into That Good Night', *Collected Poems 1934–1952* (1952), London: Dent.

Kevin Mayhew Publishing, for a quotation from Jeremy Brooks (2013), *Heaven's Morning Breaks*.

Canterbury Press, for the poem by Pádraig Ó Tuama, 'Postcards to a dead friend', in *Readings from the Book of Exile*, 2012.